Old Man
on a Green Bike

Old Man on a Green Bike

Chronicles of a Self-Serving Environmentalist

MARK CRAMER

to my grandson, Zane

who will not fall for the sedentary trap,
who will carry the flame of human
energy

First edition
ISBN: 978 1 950255 03 0

First published by Wordbound Media LLC, 2019

JUST ONE HOUR OF YOUR LIFE, GET ANOTHER HOUR FOR FREE

could spend hours and hours doing what you love and then
used-up hours returned to you at the end of your life? In
spend an hour and get another hour for free. Sounds like a
sion or a commercial scam. Romance languages don't even
or "saving" time. The whole notion of time is that you cannot
nd save it for a rainy day, or for a dying day. It just slips away
thing we can do about it.

rch from Holland published in *The American Journal of Public*
hat "Cycling prevents about 6500 deaths each year, and Dutch
lf-a-year-longer life expectancy because of cycling." This
about an hour of extended life per hour of cycling.

is research made the headlines, I'd been commuting and
bicycle for nearly two decades. I'd come back to regular
d-timer, back in 2000, not for once imagining or caring that it
ny life. In fact, if a researcher had told me that cycling
ny life instead of expanding it, I would have continued to
Paris on a bike and to take bicycle vacations in France,
gium. These commutes and excursions made me feel
oment they occurred.

longer in the future if you feel broken down right now?

statistical probability of an extra hour of life for every hour
m up on the offer. Here's what I calculate to be receiving in
is, if I fall within the statistical mean. On the average for the
cycled 10 hours per week for 40 weeks per year. More some
less other weeks, and years. These figures translate to at
dded on to my life. Being a klutz, I might negate this
e by falling in the shower and banging my head against
ing and falling down an up escalator. Both of these things
ned to me.

good right now. You're an old man or woman, you get on
enly you feel like a young man or young woman.
xtreme, every year videos circulate highlighting the
cycling for people diagnosed with Parkinson's. Indirect
lauded by bike advocates who encourage "one more
order to improve air quality. When bicycle commuters
Copenhagen, they are reducing pollution for all the
he bike riders themselves.

8

Acknowledgments

I would like to thank the following good people who have
published some of my perspectives on cycling: Lyn Eyb
(*Freewheeling France*), Sue Finley (*Thoroughbred Daily
News*), Pedro Medina León (*Suburbano.net*), Dalila Sghair
(*Roue Libre*), José Carlos Solón (*Systemic Alternatives*) and
Mark Sutton (*Cycling Industry News*), with additional
gratitude to activists in Masa Crítica, La Paz, Bolivia and MDB
(Mieux se Déplacer Bicyclette) in the Paris region, and for the
dozens of helpful readers of my manuscript, including
Roger LeBlanc, Alan Kennedy, Dr. Paul Tranter, and
especially my wife Martha. Added thanks go to Alan,
Philippe, Martha for putting up with my idiosyncrasies on
long bike rides, and my publisher Jake Mayer, for taking the
risk.

5

Contents

What if you
get all those
other words,
new-age delu
have a word
stash it away
and there's no

But 2015 resea
Health tells us
people have ha
calculated to be

By the time th
vacationing by
cycling as an ol
might extend
would shorten
wheel to work
Spain, and Be
younger at the m

Who needs to live

But here it is, the
cycled. I'll take th
bonus hours, that
past 18 years I've
weeks and years,
least 300 days a
longevity advanta
the tiles or by slip
have already happ

The point is to feel
a bike and sud
Carried to the e
positive impact of
health benefits are
bike one less car"
flood the city of
inhabitants, not just

Friends, acquaintances and readers often thank me for making the sacrifice of cycling instead of driving, in order to defend the environment and encourage others to replace fossil fuels with human energy. I respond, respectfully, that I would never think of making a sacrifice to stop climate change, because I do not believe in altruism, and in fact I've become even more self-serving in old age. I'm cycling because it makes me feel good. That's it. Now, that there's a byproduct of my actions that helps the environment, well that's superb. But don't talk to me about sacrifice.

If I were to make a sacrifice I'd be a bad role model. Jim Jones preached sacrifice and some 900 of his cult followers committed suicide. Warmongering politicians preach sacrifice in the name of The Nation and hundreds of thousands of young people volunteer for premature eradication, or end up living maimed and psychologically shattered.

I say to forget sacrifice. Sure, let's keep fossil fuels in the ground and get around on human energy, but let's do so in a sustainable way, which means in our own self-interest, for the pleasure and for the addictive feeling of well-being.

"[Commuting by bicycle is] an absolutely essential part of my day. It's mind-clearing, invigorating. I get to go out and pedal through the countryside in the early morning hours, and see life come back and rejuvenate every day as the sun is coming out."

> James Jones, former national security adviser to Barack Obama, who probably calls himself James in order to avoid any mistaken identity with the infamous Lord of Sacrifice.

But cycling is not just invigoration and rejuvenation, it's also liberation. As Ann Strong wrote in *The Minneapolis Tribune*, back in 1895: "The bicycle is just as good company as most husbands and, when it gets old and shabby, a woman can dispose of it and get a new one without shocking the entire community."

As you will experience in the subsequent pages, it's not a simple question of dumping the car, getting on a bike, and achieving long-term liberation. I've confronted formidable obstacles: manufactured, geographic, societal, logistical, biological, meteorological, psychological, and chronological, all of which are part of my story. Along the way I've made more than a few mistakes, whose lessons will help save you from falling into similar traps. I'll also make the case that no amount of technological advances will stop pollution or curtail global warming without a central role for self-serving human energy.

Finally, we've seen where courageous folks have quit their job, defied a medical problem, or said "see you next year" to their family in order cross continents on a bike in desert heat or polar cold. I love those macro-stories, and at times I'll go to some cycling extremes myself in honor of those good folks. But this book remains mostly at the haiku level of bicycle challenge, minimalist-but-memorable cycling experiences in "small extremes" that are achievable by most anyone regardless of age or athletic prowess.

I.
COMMUTING

WANTED: BICYCLE RIDER
PART-TIME, FRINGE BENEFITS

Early 2000s, Saturday morning, the air bursting into an expressionist wrestling match: cherry blossom aromas vs. diesel particles. I joined a group of mainly younger bike riders called Vélorution at Place du Châtelet, Paris, for their militant monthly gathering, where young parents deformat their kids by introducing them to organized insubordination.

Vélorution encourages bicycle commuting and other uses of the bicycle as daily transport, while advocating for a car free city. At the age of 18, swept up into the American Trance, I stopped regular bike riding and started driving a car. Back then, one calendar year was 1/18 of my life. But in 2000, the span of one year had shrunk to 1/55 of my life. I was seeking a fresh path to make up for my years of slow learning and attempting to sell the project to my more agile partner, my wife Martha, once a daring roller-skater.

I bought the Paris Municipal rhetoric that encouraged human-energy transport. City Hall told us that we could attain a type of bicycle culture prominent in cities to our north, led by Copenhagen and Amsterdam. The subtext was tantamount to: show us you are willing to commute by bike and we will provide the infrastructure in the form of cycling paths, bicycle parking and whole districts set aside for non-motorized traffic.

Within the group of bike riders mingling by the Chatelet Metro entrance, a tall young man, Tour de France physique but a scraggly beard instead of a helmet, offered to orient me. "Keep with the group," he said. "When crowds appear, we stop and chant slogans like *On avance, on avance, on n'a pas besoin d'essence*" (We go slow, we go fast, we never need a gallon of gas.)

"Show respect for pedestrians by never riding on a sidewalk. Never." He handed me a sheet of paper with the printed slogans.

"What if no human being is using the sidewalk? I asked. "Surely there are exceptions to every rule?"

"What if car drivers went into bike lanes because they didn't see a single bike at the time?" he responded. "What if you show up with your bike and a car is blocking your bike lane? And the driver says, Well I didn't see any bikes there."

Then he offered me a dream job: part-time, you choose your hours, no boss. He pointed to my bike, rented from the City of Paris. "You'll need a bike of your own," he said. "Why the rental?" "I just came here from La Paz, Bolivia, 12,000 feet above sea level, all hills and cliffs and belching old buses … So I lost the habit."

"Well, once you regain the habit with us, you could go back to Bolivia, start cycling there, and spread the message."

I resolved to bring a contour map for the next monthly outing, to show my would-be mentor that there'd be a Tour de Mars before they had a bike commuter in the world's highest capital city. For the moment, duties. "Just use your bike to commute to work," he said. "We're building an army, a whole army of silent soldiers. We're retaking our fair share of the streets."

I had English and Spanish language consulting jobs at various companies, adjunct professor gigs at two universities, and a press pass to the local horse race tracks, Longchamp, Saint-Cloud (long climb to get there) and Vincennes, where I was trying to complement my income as a scholarly horseplayer, betting against the favorite when I saw an opening.

"So you'll have different commute routes every day."

"That's what it looks like," I said. "Tell me a little more about the job, maybe tell me about the salary."

The underground economy

"Employment as we once knew it is on its way out. This is the underground economy," he explained, with great empathy. "One day they will count us in the GDP, but for the moment it's the informal economy. Next month at the Vélorution, you can tell me how many bike commuting hours you put in."

"Are you saying this pays per hour?"

"Not exactly, but if you own a car and decide to dump it, your earnings will skyrocket."

As our conversation continued, a role reversal was developing. I, the old-timer, university prof, should have been a mentor for this 22-year old Epicurus, but it was the other way around.

"Eventually you'll use your bike to go on vacation and that'll earn you a raise. Then you'll wonder why you ever made a motor trip."

Another lanky man was about to make an announcement. If my Epicurean mentor was the Yin, with beard/without helmet, his colleague with the bullhorn was the Yang, clean-shaven and sporting a sleek helmet. He called on us to get in line, double file, and we'd begin the route in slow motion. Police minders were following us on their official city bikes.

What I remember from that afternoon was a sudden stop on a Utrillo type street lined with sloping-walled medieval buildings. We stopped before a Volkswagen, which had been parked halfway on the sidewalk in order to let other cars pass by on the narrow street, thus blocking the way for pedestrians.

Suddenly eight or nine young men set their bikes against the grainy facades and began lifting the car in unison. Our two police escorts remained at a distance, spectators at the festivities. The team hoisted the car off the sidewalk and let it plop onto the pavement. They chanted something about liberating a sidewalk for pedestrians, and it rhymed in French. The anti-car sentiment was pervasive and even abrasive. But the joyful ambiance was unbeatable.

"It makes no sense," said a young dad who was riding with his toddler son in a bike seat, "that 96 percent of the fuel that goes into a car is used to propel a hunk of metal and only 4% is actually propelling the human being. One of the most inefficient uses of energy ever conceived!"

THE 13 WAYS

On Monday I bought what they call a city bike from Décathlon. Included with the bike purchase I picked out a solid lock and a thin waterproof jacket-hood-pants combination to use over my clothing in case of rain. I began commuting on Tuesday, full of apprehension. Instead of counting sheep to fall asleep at night, I counted the bike-commute obstacles I would face, in no particular order.

1. Arriving at work all sweaty on a hot day.

2. Arriving waterlogged on a rainy day.

3. Confronting an ice cold wind in the face on a winter morning.

4. Coming out of work and finding only my bike lock, sawed into two, and no sign of my bike.

5. Wheeling up to a delivery truck parked in "my" bike lane and having to swerve out into the flow of motor traffic.

6. Getting sideswiped by a turning truck.

7. Finding no path through gridlock at an intersection.

8. Getting an asthma attack from invisible diesel particles.

9. Going to a job beyond the comfortable biking distance, more than an hour away.

10. Not finding a post to hitch up my bike anywhere near the day's job.

11. Getting a flat tire: I refused to add more weight by carrying around a pump and inner tube.

12. Getting doored: how to see a parked driver opening his door right in my path if most cars have tinted windows?

13. Even if I resolve all the above 12, that would only account for some 95% of potential problems. The last 5% are particularly frightening because they include the many inevitable fluke situations, impossible to anticipate until it's [almost] too late. This is math prof. David J. Hand's law of truly large numbers: "With a large enough number of opportunities, any outrageous thing is likely to happen" (*The Improbability Principle*, p. 84).

In engineering they call this Advance Structures and Failure Analysis. I was teaching English to air traffic control engineers near Orly Airport. They explained to me how you can successfully follow all the rules to avoid accidents but that it's impossible to engineer away a very small percentage of failures that fall within the fluke category. In such cases you can only do the preventive engineering after a fluke crash occurs, at which time you study the why. I figured my students had some serious credentials, since I needed a security badge to get into their complex. So I listened carefully to what they had to say.

Without realizing it, I had already learned something about Failure Analysis, from horse race handicapping. At least 95% of the information needed to choose a good bet is readily available to the studious handicapper. But the remaining 5% accounts for more valuable longshot winners than the entire 95% of more obvious variables. There are only three possible reasons why a low- return favorite wins a race but within the 5% fluke category, you find hundreds of reasons why a longshot can win.

Like air-traffic experts, longshot players study these hundreds of reasons after each crash. But in my cycling, I did not want to wait for after a crash in order to learn how to anticipate a potential danger. So, I rejoiced at a chance to learn more about failure engineering.

During this period, while I was getting paid to learn what I desperately needed to know, the perfectly designed Concorde, the Titanic of the air, crashed spectacularly during a Charles de Gaulle takeoff because of a freak piece of debris on the runway that flew up and precisely hit the part of the fuel tank that was nearest to the surface of the fuselage. One hundred seventeen people died in the explosion. This accident fell within my category 13, the last 5%, the flukes that could not be planned against ...until after they happened. (See Postscript at the end of this book: *9 Random Mishap Scenarios: Advance Structure Failure Analysis.*)

In my counting ritual, I usually fell asleep before the number thirteen fluke category. Reaching (13) meant possible sleep deprivation since with a little imagination, I could anticipate hundreds of Concorde-like scenarios: a piece of broken bottle on the bike path whose curvature when in contact with my bike wheel would send it spiraling up, precisely into my forehead, for example. It was essential for me to at least anticipate how I could overcome the more bizarre fluke scenarios. The Concorde tragedy is engraved in history. But if and when I die from a fluke cycling accident, my story will rapidly fade into oblivion.

15

When a job becomes an extended coffee break

My days were composed of taking a bike ride, stopping off for a job that included a cup of espresso, then riding home. As one of the slowest espresso drinkers in recorded history, my last sip usually transpired in the waning moments of the whatever session I was conducting. I'd always wanted jobs that seemed like coffee breaks, and now I had them.

A month and 350 commuting kilometers later, I arrived at the next Vélorution, same start at Châtelet, but this one was going to end at Porte de Bagnolet, east edge of Paris, near our apartment. My "employer" was nowhere to be seen. I ordered myself to not panic. I gave the description of the man who had hired me to his colleague, a guy named Philippe.

"Oh, that's Guillaume. He's a philosopher. He speaks in metaphors."

"What do you mean, metaphors?"

"We all work for Guillaume," Philippe said, setting aside the bullhorn on a hedge. "We're silent soldiers, recapturing our fair share of the streets, and we're also bike messengers, spreading the word about clean air, democratic streets, and the only truly renewable energy: human energy."

He waved his lanky arms as if he were speaking to an audience of 50,000. "Compare the cost of a bike with the cost of a car," he said, to me alone. "We don't pay for gas, we got free parking and no toll ways, we don't pay for license plates, we don't pay for insurance, and maintenance is cheap compared to an automobile. By not using a car, we're making $8,000 dollars per year."

Well-versed in all transportation literature, he wondered how, as an American, I had not even read the U.S. Bureau of Labor Statistics!

Bicycle commuting health insurance

"And the fringe benefits?" I asked.

"Bike commuting is like health insurance, as opposed to medical insurance. With bicycle commuting we have a 41% lower risk of dying from cardiovascular, cancer and other causes. Check *The British Medical Journal*!"

At the end of the ride, by the Périphérique ring road at Porte de Bagnolet, known as "Europe's Crossroads," I participated in a collective applause followed by a lifting of our bikes, as if we'd won the Tour de France, culminated by punchy messages from exhilarated speakers. A young woman, zebra helmet in hand, explained that if we could reach a critical mass of bicycle commuters in Paris, this criminal air pollution (she pointed menacingly to the Périphérique freeway) would be reduced and Paris would become breathable, "for ALL people, not just bike riders!"

Until that moment, I'd been turned off by some environmentalists, the ones who mentioned the need to "make sacrifices" and the ones who spoke gravely about the upcoming apocalypse. I had no problem with the flawed human species becoming extinct, though I would not say this in front of my grandson.

But the bicycle militants I'd shared two Saturday afternoons with gave the impression that environmentalism could be fun. I resolved to continue as a silent soldier and bike messenger. But that depended first on resolving some serious logistics problems that were putting my life in danger, like car doors that might swing open in front of me, motorcyclists hogging their way into bike lanes, and trucks making sudden right turns that crossed directly into my path.

The 13 Ways

On one particular night, before falling asleep, instead of merely counting the 13 obstacles, I began composing the lyrics for *13 Ways to Purge your Perils*, based on Paul Simon's *50 Ways to Leave Your Lover,* in which the singer-composer refers to his "struggle to be free," moaning and crooning that you should "sleep on it tonight / I believe in the morning / you'll begin to see the light." Simon Says made it seem easy: "Make a new plan, Stan" and "Hop on the bus, Gus."

I dozed off to "Find a new road, Joad" (to escape gridlock), "Take off the seat, Pete" (to dissuade a potential bike thief), and for a scorching hot day, "Take extra clothes, Mose" in honor of the late great Mose Allison, who likely influenced Paul Simon's style in *50 Ways.*

In the morning I began to see the light. So did the Municipality, which was increasing the number of bike lanes and parking rails, and widening bus-bike corridors. As my confidence grew, I began to see that bike commuting was just the first part of a larger transformation. Sooner or later I would need to experiment with using the bicycle on vacations. Paris is a small city with a boxed-in dollhouse feeling for some of us who situate ourselves in "the struggle to be free."

Paris once had a medieval rampart, most of which was destroyed. But a psychological rampart remained. I needed to be assured that there was something beyond, reachable by bike. Or was I a manipulated character in a *Truman Show* (based on Philip K. Dick's *Time Out of Joint*), within an invisible-walled Disneyland of Culture, with no way out.

I had no idea how long it would take me to wheel out of Paris and its sprawling suburbs in order to reach the authentic French countryside, without getting contained in what Fox News famously called "no-go zones." But that was thinking ahead. First I had to work out the 13 ways.

PELTED: THE SHOELESS PROFESSOR

In cities where bike lanes are not always protected and streets do not always have bike lanes, getting doored was the number one theoretical obstacle to safe bike commuting. But the most immediate threat came from the weather. Bicycle commuters in cold-winter cities like Copenhagen and Minneapolis have proven they can outsmart the weather. (A combination of good cycling infrastructure and the right clothing and equipment keeps the percentage of commutes by bicycle in Copenhagen at above 40% and allows for an increase in Minneapolis to above 5%).

The grungy but sporty bicycle philosopher "employer" insisted that I could cycle under all circumstances. But if it felt like winter in Bangor, Maine, or summer in scorching Bahrain, I feared I might wimp out and take the train.

How many steamy Bangladeshi summers are there in the world, how many wind-whipped Chicago winters, where deterministic weather transforms a few blocks of cycling into an extreme sport? I'd rather deal with steep hills in the Pyrenees than flat rides in the oil rich Gulf States, where "the harsh climate, which discourages outdoor sports and even walking around outside" (Barry, *Euromonitor International*) fuels an obesity epidemic.

In fact, of the 20 countries with the highest obesity rates, 19 of them also had extremely high average temperatures (above 25 C), including all the Gulf States. Of the top 20 obesity leaders, the only lower-temperature outlier was the USA (ranked 19), with an average of 8.55 C. But within the USA, eight of the ten states ranked highest in obesity were also among those with the hottest average temperatures, including Texas, Louisiana, Mississippi, and Alabama. Without denying an essential role of eating and drinking habits as a cause of a number of weight-related medical conditions, it's clear that extreme hot climate thwarts purposeful physical activities such as walking and cycling.

I was hell-bent on outsmarting the most punitive weather adversaries, which accounted for four of my 13 commuting obstacles, by employing clever strategies.

When the heat assaults, wear a tee-shirt and pack my work clothes in my backpack, kept on the rear bike rack, not on my back, to avoid sweating. Leave home early, ahead of the heat, riding at a slower pace. Upon arriving at work, scoot to the bathroom, freshen up and change clothes. In the clutches of bone-crunching cold, Minnesota outranks hot Mississippi in percentage of commuter trips by bike. Cold is more manageable than heat.

With aging, though, I'm becoming cowardly. To outsmart the cold, I wear multiple levels on top, plus scarf, and double leg coverage. I'm embarrassed to have once mocked the "snow birds" who abandon New York for Florida in the winter. Partway to work, I begin peeling off the levels, as the cycling itself warms me up. In the cold I imagine cycling in Kuwait in 110 degrees F and I make a truce with my adversary.

In the battering wind, a strong gust can whip me out of my lane into the path of a truck. If the sycamores outside our dining room window are swaying violently in gusts of plus 80 km (50 mph), I consider leaving the bike home. If the wind will be at my back on the way to work, I won't mind confronting it later, head on, on the way back home.

Pollution. On days when Airparif (the pollution measurement office) publishes a danger alert and public transportation is thus declared free of charge by the mayor to entice motorists off the road, breathing in the micro-particles that come from diesel fuel emissions is not worth the risk. These sneaky micro-particles will even penetrate a mask. But after all is said and done, we are spoiled in Paris, where it is a rare day when any weather factor decomposes into the red zone.

The most complex weather decision involves the rain. Rain here is usually intermittent, and the stronger it pours, the less likely it will last. Therefore, the rain should not stop me from cycling. When the deluge is unleashed, just pull over and wait under cover (a bus stop, a building corridor). But my strategy did not help on one Saturday morning when, after the first five minutes in the saddle, I realized that a thinking person would have left the bike home. It was the type of relentless rain I'd once experienced south of Portland, Oregon, where flooding washed out the Interstate.

Now I was teaching a Saturday morning university class from 9am to 11am, at the science university, Paris 6, at Jussieu, near the Jardin des Plantes. I was the only language prof to volunteer for Saturdays. When it comes to work, I opt for the easier alternative. Saturday groups involved the most mature and advanced students, those who worked during the week and took pleasure in lively Saturday morning interactions.

My job was to coach these students on giving presentations in English and writing articles within their specialties. I was getting paid to learn from grad students in physics and biology, about neuron-stimulating subjects, part of my insurance policy against Alzheimer's. In this particular stormy Saturday, the group of 16 was composed of masters and doctoral physics students in fluid mechanics or robotics.

My waterproof pants, jacket and hood failed to ward off *la flotte*. In order to punch through the rain, I listened to Stormy Weather. I say "listen" but I don't use ear phones. I've memorized the versions by Billie Holiday, Ella Fitzgerald and Etta James, and I could hear them clearly through the downpour. By the time I arrived, I was especially drenched at the ankles and feet. My houseplants would have died had they absorbed as much moisture as my shoes.

Having taken precautions, I'd stashed an extra pair of socks and shirt in a plastic bag within my backpack, but what good are dry socks in soaked shoes?

The campus was being rebuilt to eliminate asbestos infestation, and I was housed in a temporary but comfortable two-story building. As the only teacher on the second floor, I had the keys to my castle.

I'd barely arrived on time, so before I went to the bathroom to change and recompose, I divided my students into three separate classrooms according to group-managed assignments. Meanwhile, back in the bathroom, I came to the realization that I had no choice but to leave the soaked shoes on a windowsill and show up shoeless to conduct the class.

No fretting about some unsympathetic French student spreading the word that he had a shoeless professor. (I'd been told that some French people are judgmental on the grounds of form rather than content, and entering a classroom shoeless is a flaw in form.)

I was working as an adjunct, with no contract. The administration needed no pretext to not rehire me for the following semester. But I was willing to risk losing the gig long term in order to enjoy my two-hour class in comfort, in other words, shoeless, in warm socks.

Well-being begins in the feet.

WHAT WILL HAPPEN FIRST: WILL ROBOTS BECOME HUMANIZED, OR WILL HUMANS BECOME ROBOTS?

The first group of five students was finishing their letters to the editor. They'd chosen to respond to controversial science articles from *The New York Times, Time Magazine* and *Scientific American*, and were crafting 150-word letters. (From time to time, my students' letters would get published!) In Wikipedia style, they corrected each others' writing.

Group two, comprised of six robotics students, prepared a presentation on *What is going to happen first? Will robots become humanized or will humans become robots?*

The third group included five fluid mechanics students. They were preparing a presentation in response to claims by 911 conspiracy theorists that there had been controlled demolitions of the two main World Trade Center towers, as well as Building 7, which was not even hit by a plane but nevertheless collapsed. The anti-war movement, in which I participated, was becoming infested by conspiracy freaks. Avoiding any leading questions, I hoped my students would provide scientific arguments to debunk the conspiracy claims.

These were future Einsteins, unconcerned about surface aesthetics

In the bathroom I'd dried off my feet and ankles with paper towels. I took a deep breath with a micro-meditation, in appreciation of a newly acquired pleasure of dry socks. No cold beer on a steamy afternoon can compare with warm dry socks on a soggy morning. In visiting with each student group, it soon became apparent that my future Einsteins were entirely unconcerned about the surface aesthetics of a shoeless professor.

After their 20 minutes of preparation time, I relocked two of the classrooms and we gathered together in the third room of my Saturday-morning chateau. I expected some healthy debate from the robotics group, but instead they reached a unanimous conclusion: that human beings would become robots long before robots were humanized. One of the students assured me that "It's already happening!"

"The cell phone and earphones have become integral parts of the body," he said, "and that's just the surface!" I'd expected the opposite conclusion from robotics students. I played Devil's Advocate. "When I ride a bike, I'm also tethered to a machine," I said. "But the energy is controlled by you and only you," they answered, "with no outside electronic forces rewiring your neurons." In other words, riding a bike reaffirms my control over my own human biology.

To my satisfaction, the fluid mechanics group proved, beyond doubt, that the World Trade Center buildings collapsed because of the fires, triggered by both direct crashes and flying debris. They partly blamed the atypical architectural structure of the buildings for allowing the flames to spread so quickly and for the buildings to pancake. Here was another example of what the air-traffic-control engineers called Advanced Structure Failure Analysis. (Conspiracy freaks would soon brush aside the objective information provided by my students. Like good sectarians, they believed only what they wanted and needed to believe.)

I rode back home in wet shoes and a clinging wet jacket. Rather than relinquishing to the vengeful Rain Gods, I resolved to look for the right foot and ankle covering at an all-purpose bike shop. Guillaume, my bicycle philosopher employer, had insisted that cycling was possible anywhere and at any time. Even if there were no real income forthcoming, if I ever found him again, I'd demand payment for this one pulverizing Saturday morning.

Eventually I was obligated to abandon this teaching gig because French free-tuition public universities had a mandatory retirement age of 66. Age had stopped me from continuing this one fulfilling job, but so far there were no age restrictions on my newest profession: bicycle commuter.

DOORED! BAM

After riding twice with Vélorution, the Parisian version of the worldwide movement, Critical Mass, I got it: we cyclists were supposed to be the Good Guys. We defended pedestrians against the motor vehicle occupation of our cities, and we defended bus drivers, users of public transportation and all citizens, because everyone has to breathe the air. People did not have to ride a bike to be on our side. They only had to stop driving a car. So did that make car drivers the enemy?

Not according to Ivan Illich, one of the great bicycle advocates, author of the polemical *Deschooling Society* and other books that challenged preconceived ideas. In *Energy and Equity*, Illich refers to "energy thresholds beyond which power corrupts." Referring to voracious energy consumption as a parallel to overeating, Illich warned that, past a certain output or speed, "mechanical transformers of mineral fuels excluded people from the use of their metabolic [human] energy and forced them to become captive consumers of conveyance" [especially the automobile but also other forms of high-speed transport].

The driver or passenger "in a world monopolized by transport becomes a harassed, overburdened consumer of distances whose shape and length he can no longer control." Along a Seine River bike path in which I was rolling past the gridlocked cars to my left, I wondered how many of these drivers would have opted for a different form of transportation if they'd had the freedom of choice. "It's all well and good that you can commute by bike," said one friend who was a regular driver. "I can't afford the high rents in Paris, where I work, so I had no choice but to move to the suburbs, far beyond cycling distance."

The lanky Vélorution philosopher, my "employer," had warned me to avoid conflict with obnoxious drivers. However, my first discovery in the initial weeks of bicycle commuting was how much empathy I received from car drivers, just by establishing eye contact, even at moments while we were vying for the same scarce street space.

The real enemy, as I discerned from Illich, was the complex web of energy industries. "Beyond a certain speed," he explained, "no one can save time without forcing another to lose it... Beyond a certain velocity, passengers [including drivers] become consumers of other people's time, and accelerating vehicles become a means of effecting a net transfer of life-time."

I mulled over these Illich lines just as accelerating motorcyclists, in order to avoid the gridlock, leached into my bike lane like water finding the quickest groove. I stopped on the Left Bank across from the Notre-Dame cathedral and asked a traffic cop why it was that she and her colleagues were allowing motorcycles in the bike lanes.

She flashed a maternal smile. "Désolée monsieur, there are just too many of them for us to have any control." I decided to exclude motor vehicle drivers from my road rage, channeling it instead to what Illich called "the radical monopoly of industry."

Getting doored

But car drivers were not totally exempt from my potential road rage. From the outset, I learned from bicycle activists to always look right at parked cars to make sure no door was opening just as I passed. Drivers in parked cars are less attentive than the ones on the road.

Even when you watch to the right, you cannot really anticipate a door opening until it's too late, since most cars have tinted windows. So the real answer to avoid The Big Door is to ride well away from the open door distance of parked cars, the door zone to your right, even if that puts you in the middle of car traffic.

I was pulling up to a red light on Rue de Charenton, attentively looking to my right (while passing idling cars on my left) in order to take my safe and proper place ahead of the first row of stopped cars (and put me within the eyesight of drivers waiting for the green light). This advanced position prevents the bike rider from getting sideswiped by a car turning right.

A passenger decided to get out on his right (my left, where I was not looking), just as I was riding by.

I smashed into the door and went down. As I brushed off my elbow and hand bruises, both the frightened driver and his passenger emerged from their two-ton hunk of steel and plastic, helped me up and apologized profusely, checking my wounds, and offering to take me to nearby Hôpital Saint-Antoine. Clearly the passenger had not followed the traffic code, in getting out from a middle lane. In non-litigious France, I was not about to file a law suit over a scraped elbow.

Nor was the second time I was doored a text-book case, and to this very day I wonder if even the most seasoned cyclist could have avoided it. I was cycling up Rue de Clichy after sunset in a theater district, approaching a taxi that was stopped at least three yards from the curb, partially blocking the oncoming traffic from behind. There was no reason at all to suspect that the driver would open his door in mid-traffic. And he didn't. But from behind him, a passenger, a glitzy older woman dressed in ostentatious black, had been too lazy to slide over to her right and get out where she was supposed to: curbside.

Instead, she decided ("decided" is giving her the benefit of the doubt that she was actually thinking) to get out into the traffic, just as I was cycling by. The door opened and I crashed right into it. The lady got out as if nothing had happened, walking around what could have been my corpse in order to stand in line at the theater entrance.

Strangely, I only remember the fright of seeing the door open, but not the fall itself! This is very good news. It says that if I die in a fall, I will not really be there when it happens, fulfilling the yearning of Woody Allen, who declared he was not afraid of dying but did not want to be there when it happened.

I do remember being on the ground, wondering where I would find the bruises. The taxi driver emerged, raising his hands in frustration. He had no idea that a dumb passenger would exit his car on the traffic side. "It's still your responsibility," I reasoned, looking up at the galaxy of theater lights from my unreserved seat on the pavement.

He helped me up. It was a miracle that I had no injury, not even a scratch, and even more miraculously I was not hit by any drivers swerving around me from behind. Knowing that anything can happen on gridless Parisian streets, I decided to compose an Ode to Parisian Drivers.

The Sting

That was a bizarre incident. But the third time I was doored wins the Oscar for the Most Peculiar Dooring Incident, and I had the starring role! I was cycling up Avenue de Clichy (not to be confused with Rue de Clichy), singing a song and rolling along, feeling 100% protected by the Paris police. I was following two bicycle police officers, the three of us in single file, as we passed a yellow postal truck.

The first bicycle cop passed the postal truck, the second rider passed the postal truck, and following the police formation, I too began to pass. But at that moment, the postal driver opened his door ...Bam, I went down. To add insult to injury, the two cops I'd been entrusting my life to, stopped their bikes, looked back and grinned... as if this had been their successful sting operation. I don't remember their faces but I do remember their big grins.

The only things in common between these three unpredictable dooring incidents is that they all "fell" within my fluke category 13: Advance Structure and Failure Analysis. Of course there is an engineering solution: it's called The Protected Bike Lane.

Within the 5% fluke category, potential accident scenarios multiply geometrically, outnumbering all accidents within the other 95% scenarios. The Protected Bike Lane removes the dooring danger from the realm of inevitable failure. With it, there are no parked cars to the right of the cyclists, only the curb, and to the cyclist's left are concrete curbs or barriers, or flexible plastic posts that separate the bike rider from the "door zone" of parked cars.

The USA lagged behind Europe in protected lanes because the American traffic code considered the bicycle as just another type of vehicle, subject to the same rules as cars. American cyclists did not need their own infrastructure, just knowledge of Department of Motor Vehicle codes. But most folks do not feel comfortable as "vehicular cyclists" and as a consequence, the USA remains behind Europe in percentage of bike commutes.

The American bicycle-commuter revolution began with activist groups demanding protected bike lanes. One of the hundreds of advocacy groups, People For Bikes, says that more than 100 American cities now have at least one protected lane. New York was one of the first to implant protected lanes on a massive scale, since 2007, with around 100 miles of safe lanes, and the share of NYC bicycle commuters has risen accordingly. (see Chapter 11, CAN WE TRAVEL FASTER ON A BIKE THAN IN A CAR?

With protected lanes, none of my dooring incidents would have occurred. Furthermore, the safety factor from protected lanes expands beyond its objective infrastructural reality. Protected lanes create a secondary effect: an increasing number of bike commuters. Once past a critical mass on city streets, bicycle riders are no longer outliers. Car drivers take more precautions, knowing that at any given point they will be sharing the street with non-motorized transport.

It's important to note that in many countries, dooring incidents are considered the fault of the vehicle occupant. According to cycling specialist, journalist Laura Laker, dooring is "a criminal offense, punishable with a £1,000 fine" in the UK (see *The Guardian Bike Blog*, 19 Oct 2018).

I'm not sure I'd have liked to see the perpetrators in my own door attacks hit with such a punishment, not even the glitzy lady in the theater district who got out of the taxi on the traffic side of the car and then stepped over my potentially dead body. There is a solution to avoid dooring, which Laker refers to as The Dutch Reach: "using the opposite arm to open a door," which forces the driver to look behind to see what's approaching.

MASK OR HELMET?

These two safety measures need to be discussed together. They should be of equal importance but one gets all the hype and the other is ignored. During my first seven years of bicycle commuting, I fell seven times (including the three dooring incidents referenced in the previous chapter). Not once did I injure my head. In the next 10 years, perhaps thanks to my slow but sure learning, my number of falls decreased from 7 to 0. That is an anecdote, not a statistic.

The diagnostic article, "Why it makes sense to bike without a helmet" (Howie Chong, 24 Feb 2014, is much more nuanced than its provocative title. The author begins with a qualifier: "Let's first get one thing out of the way: if you get into a serious accident, wearing a helmet will probably save your life."

According to a 1989 study in *The New England Journal of Medicine*, riders with helmets [following serious accidents] had an "85% reduction in their risk of head injury and an 88% reduction in their risk of brain injury." But then, the author indulges in "a broader look, comparing cyclists' head trauma risk, referring to studies from San Diego, France and Australia showing that more people were hospitalized after walking down the street than were un-helmeted cyclists.

Chong referred to an article by Australian researcher D.L. Robinson: "Head Injuries and Bicycle Helmet Laws," in *Accident Analysis and Prevention* (July, 1996. On the surface, it looks slightly more dangerous to be a pedestrian or car occupant than an un-helmeted bike rider. Until now, most studies on cycling risk have been flawed. They do not consider, for example, the setting, speed, and mode of cycling. We need a comparison of risk between cities with good networks of protected bike lanes and those that lack a safety infrastructure. We need to compare dangerous forms of cycling, such as mountain biking, with commuting at less than 10 miles per hour.

The study was published at the time Australia had adopted a mandatory bicycle helmet law. According to this same study, "...the greatest effect of the helmet law was not to encourage cyclists to wear helmets, but to discourage cycling," not a good sign for public health officials who are trying to encourage active transportation. That same study suggests that a mandatory helmet law for motor vehicle occupants could save seventeen times more people from death and serious head injury than a similar law for cyclists.

Chong goes on to ask an objectively legitimate question that would be scoffed at in most cultures: "If the reason we are supposed to wear helmets while biking is to prevent serious head injury on the off-chance we get into an accident, then why is it socially acceptable for pedestrians and drivers to go about bare-headed? Why has cycling been singled out as an activity in need of head protection?"

Risk of head injury per million hours traveled:	• Cyclist - 0.41
	• Pedestrian - 0.80
	• Motor vehicle occupant - 0.46
	• Motorcyclist - 7.66

To wear or not to wear

Here's a picture worth the thousand words. The influential French Federation of Bicycle Users (FUB) distributes a pamphlet, *Bikes, bus, trucks, let's coexist!* The pamphlet has 8 color photos and one cartoon with technical examples of how cyclists should ride to avoid a crash with a truck. In each of these illustrations, the cyclist is NOT wearing a helmet. And this is a safety brochure! The next time well-meaning folks get on my case for not wearing a helmet, I'll show them this pamphlet.

Nevertheless, I would never advise a future bike rider to not wear a helmet. Without evaluating riding skills, maturity level or the cycling infrastructure of his or her city, it would be irresponsible on my part to chime in. A daughter and a granddaughter of mine have cycled with me in France and California. Both have athletic talents that I lack. Yet they perceive a risk in cycling without a helmet and it's their choice to wear one.

When asked why I choose to NOT wear a helmet. My long-winded response:

1. I choose routes that avoid dangerous traffic situations, both urban and rural, even though this adds kilometers to my ride;

2. My urban commuting speed is 10 mph or less, which greatly reduces the danger of head injury if a fall does occur;

3. I have read the statistical research showing that motor vehicle drivers, when overtaking bike riders, give helmeted cyclists significantly less space than they give cyclists without a helmet;

4. Safety in numbers: mandatory bike helmets discourage many people from bike commuting. The fewer the cyclists on the road, the more vulnerable they become.

My granddaughter does perilous aerial dancing without a helmet but chooses to wear a helmet when cycling. Wearing a helmet is her subjective choice. That's fine. But why are we having this helmet discussion at all when air pollution, a more insidious and immediate danger to cyclists, is virtually ignored by public safety authorities. I would not want this to happen, but any municipality with above-average air pollution that chooses to make helmets mandatory for bike riders should, by its own logic, also require masks.

A mask is even more uncomfortable than a helmet. I've worn a mask on hotter summer days when the air quality was poor, and no matter how hard I tried, I could not get used to it. Learning that fine diesel particles are not stopped by the mask was the clincher: no mask for me. The long-term public health risks coming from inactivity (refraining from bicycle commuting because of air pollution) may be greater than the risks of cycling in the foul air without a mask, though neither alternative is desirable.

In the country where I reside, "air pollution kills 48,000 people a year," according to a 21 June 2016 report on Radio France International, with 34,000 of these deaths avoidable. A large percentage of these deaths can be linked to motor vehicle emissions. Automobile manufacturers are required by law to install seat belts and airbags, for the safety of their own customers. By the same logic, you could argue for the enactment of measures requiring car manufacturers to protect the victims of car emissions by supplying anti-pollution masks to the billions of pedestrians exposed to the mortal car fumes. Such "externalities" should be included in the cost of an automobile.

Eventually, car manufacturers will be seen in the same light as cigarette companies, having wantonly spread a potent addiction. Ads for cigarette companies have been banned but the private automobile continues to be hyped in the media. The Marlboro man never lost his job. They just changed his clothes and put him in a freewheeling car next to a beautiful woman, with breathtaking scenery and no traffic. As Illich noted, beyond a certain velocity, the freedom of a car driver becomes the consumer of other people's time and health.

As a former Los Angeles resident I can testify that freeways grant drivers the freedom to deposit soot on our apartment windows, and to blight our neighborhoods, rendering them unwalkable. "Where are the people on the streets?" ask European visitors.

To compete in the So Cal job market, I'm required to dedicate a large chunk of my work hours to buying and maintaining a car that can compete on those miserable freeways and get me to work. And if I took a bus instead? When it comes to your reputation in LA, you'd rather be spotted in a porn shop than on a bus. Folks who use public transportation are the Untouchables. And God help you if you get caught as a pedestrian on one of many streets with no sidewalks. Better walk fast because the Neighborhood Watch will call the cops on you!

Whoever invented the wheel, he or she would be appalled to see such a great invention evolving into a private vehicle in which members of formerly pedestrian species are now tethered to a two-ton hunk of metal and plastic, immobilized and sedentary.

Secondhand smoke and secondhand fumes

They barred smoking from restaurants because of the dangers of secondhand smoke. What about the dangers of secondhand sulfur dioxide, secondhand nitrogen oxide, secondhand carbon monoxide and secondhand fine metallic particles? Where are the warning labels on new cars?

As a user of non-motorized transport, I deserve priority on the streets of my city. If they do not give it to me, I'll take it anyway- even if I have to carry an inhaler in my backpack.

Why not find a humane way to remove fossil fuel "smokers" from public space by providing car drivers with attractive alternatives for getting around? Don't blame the drivers themselves. For the most part they live in a society that offers them no viable transportation alternatives.

MY MYSTERIOUS EMPLOYER

At the dodgy Bastille roundabout I was vying for space with another cyclist. It turned out to be Guillaume, my mentor. We decided to stop for a beer on the narrow cobblestone Rue de Lappe, a pedestrian oasis free of car fumes. We locked our bikes to a post and took a sidewalk table. He asked me if I was still biking all my commutes.

"I finally got it," I said. "You weren't really offering me a gig. That's fine with me. I've always been shitty at grasping symbolism."

"I told you we're in the underground economy. If you keep doing something you like, eventually someone will pay you for it. And if not, you still did something you liked."

I learned he was a grad student. His choice of thesis, on social inequalities in the age of Amazon, was an intellectual preference, void of practical considerations. He assured me he'd survive in a world where studies other than finance and information technology no longer tracked you on a path to employment.

"Like you explained," I said, "we have a cause."

"Beware of the word cause," he said. "You don't want to sound like an altruist. There's no such thing as altruism. If there were a true altruist, he'd have to be extremely selfish. There's nothing wrong with legitimate self-interest."

He savored a sip of Stella Artois. Like many French icons, for example Jacques Brel, Herge (*Tintin*'s creator), whodunit writer Georges Simenon and even Johnny Hallyday, Stella Artois was a product of Belgium.

"Statistics show that when the number of cyclists rises, cycling deaths or serious injuries decline," he added. "So we ride for ourselves, to feel good, and the collateral result is that we save lives. That's the concept of critical mass, and it's not altruistic." Guillaume took his time, both sipping beer and preaching leisurely to his one-man choir.

"Besides, I have another job for you that won't get you an immediate paycheck. We're having a public symposium with Serge Latouche and two other speakers. We need a guest provoker on stage to ask them probing questions."

I'd read articles by Latouche. He was a French Ivan Illich. Illich wrote about De-schooling and Latouche did Degrowth, an alternative socio-economic system. I'd failed to ask any tough questions of Ivan Illich 38 years earlier when sitting right across the table from him: a squandered opportunity! Latouche was the second chance I'd never thought I'd get.

"But why me? I write about travel and gambling. That hardly makes me the right guest." A gotcha look emerged between the whiskers of his scraggly beard. "Ah, gambling! Latouche's book *le Pari de la Decroissance* translates, *Gambling on Degrowth*."

Guillaume's thought process involved hidden neural connections. Even when cycling across the Bastille roundabout, his subconscious remained wide awake, if that's possible. I asked him to elaborate.

"The first time we met at the Velorution event, you told me you lived in a modest apartment near Porte de Bagnolet, but that you'd once lived in your own home with a back yard in California. You said you once had three cars in the family and now you don't even own one. You told me you felt liberated by cutting out the clutter. We can introduce you as someone who has actually lived a path to sustainable degrowth. You'd be questioning the speakers from a perspective of authenticity." Should I have felt flattered or was I being recruited as the fool on the hill? "Don't even mention keeping fossil fuels in the ground," he said. "It'll be implicit in your story."

So I was the implicitor, a specimen, a visceral being unaware of his own discoveries. Needing to sound more scholarly than a fool on the hill, I summoned up an idea from Illich and reworked it: "Don't worry, I won't touch that slogan or any other abstraction," I assured him. "When you defeat the fossil fuel companies, you may only pave the way for a new crew of mafioso running the wind and solar industries, prolonging the illusion of limitless consumption."

A fresh breeze blew a napkin off our table. A ragged young homeless man picked up the soiled napkin, placed it on the table, and held out his hand. I took a sweet apple out of my backpack and offered it to him. With a snide grin, moving the palm of his hand in a back and forth motion, he declined, as if he were a referee and I'd just earned a red card. He stumbled away. Even sprawling in his chair, Guillaume retained the profile of an agile athlete. Yet there was also a resemblance to the old professor in the Italian film, *The Organizer.* "The CEOs of Exxon and Total have long been aware that they're fucking over future generations," he said. "So our only choice, even if deterministic forces somehow generate our actions, is to oppose the bastards."

I'd strolled on Rue de Lappe back in 1991, before it became a gentrified and pedestrian haven. I perceived both positive and negative effects of gentrification, but was unable to separate the two. The seedier Rue de Lappe of 1991 was enticing in its own way and the rent was lower, but cars streamed by back then, depositing soot in the lungs of the local inhabitants.

Wishing to stick around and maybe decipher this cobblestoned gentrification process, I proposed another round of Belgian beer before we departed on our separate ways. He declined, reminding me that I wasn't riding alone, that I was part of a movement, and that the drinking-and-driving limitations applied to bike riders as well as to motorists. I wondered whether this movement I was a part of contained a strain of Calvinist austerity even while we proclaimed joie de vivre.

NAKED ON A BIKE

On October 17, 2014, Velorution came up with a strategy for confronting the Paris International Motor Show, on closing day of the car industry's annual two weeks of glory. Velorutionaires gathered on the esplanade in front of the convention center, Porte de Versailles.

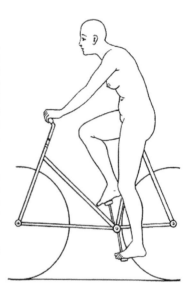

In order to denounce the vulnerability of cyclists who navigate through the dangerous automobile empire, Velorution members decided to ride naked. Derived from Portland, Oregon's daring World Naked Bike Ride, which attracts thousands of bicycle protesters each year, the event is also a protest against oil dependency.

Velorution labeled the Motor Show the "Convention of World Self-Destruction," where "car drivers celebrated the phantom of their all-powerful dominion" and "their stage setting of male domination over women reduced to the status of objects."

I mentioned this event to my wife Martha, and before I could finish, she chimed in: "You're not going to that thing!"

Once a month we each have the chance to exercise our veto. This was her veto. She'd wasted it, though, since I hadn't even planned to go. I'd lost contact with Velorution, having joined a bike group with more presence in my neighborhood: MDB (*Mieux se Deplacer a Bicyclette*).

"Okay, I'm not going, but surely you can see the symbolism of being naked on a bike," I explained, this time able to finish my sentence.

My Socratic partner responded with a question. "Do you think an SUV salesman would be capable of grasping the symbolism?"

I explained that this was a way for velorution to break through the fossil-fueled media embargo. "Yes," she said, "as the object of ridicule!"

One of the bikes carried a sign, *L'indecence c'est 'essence,* a perfect rhyme that translates: "indecency is gasoline." "We are naked and fragile when riding in traffic against the flow of cars," declared one participant. Perhaps the most symbolic image was the mostly undressed woman who nevertheless wore a face mask as protection against car fumes.

As Martha had suspected, newspaper coverage of the demonstration was not so warm to the symbolism. One scornful article chose to highlight the fact that only 20 cyclists showed up and that they were shuffled away by the police for not having gotten a written permit from the Prefecture de Police.

Their five minutes of semi-naked glory exemplified how unattractive is the unclothed human body. As a "textile" (one who wears clothing), I'd once seen such grotesquery when stumbling upon a nudist colony during a hike in the province of Quebec.

When chimpanzees look at us from the other side of the zoo cage, they must cringe. Nevertheless, this event might have been one of Velorution's most successful. This group of bicycle militants is often ignored by the press, but this time any Parisian reading a newspaper got to know the goals of Velorution, perhaps for the first time. They blew it, though, by not hiring some professional models. I know, you say, that's a pact with the devilish system. But I'd have chipped in to pay for a few porn star cyclists.

I was not sure just how naked and fragile I felt when cycling on the streets of Paris. Car drivers here seemed more tolerant than those in Los Angeles, Las Vegas and Livonia, Michigan. Nevertheless, I had felt much safer riding on sensibly laid out streets of Barcelona and Amsterdam. The angular, gridless asymmetry of Paris along with the discontinuity of bike paths and anarchistic roundabouts give this city a feeling of uncertainty. As explained in a previous chapter, getting doored was my primary sense of vulnerability. But three other precarious scenarios made me feel naked: left turns in traffic with no arrows, intersections when you're in the blind spot of the vehicle outside you (which may decide to cross your path for a turn), and when a delivery truck is parked in your bike lane, forcing you to swerve out into traffic to get by him.

This last one, the intruding delivery truck, is especially tough for old-timers with creaky necks. The first time this happened to me, I had trouble turning my stiff neck to make sure I could swerve out safely. Since then, I do neck stretches before leaving home on my bike.

Whatever the new booby traps I expected to encounter, it was apparent that bike commuting did not strip me down to my frightful animal innards .

There were enough statistics to suggest that walking might be even more dangerous than cycling ("Mile for mile, it's more dangerous to be a pedestrian than it is to be a cyclist," according to *fullfact.org* and *The Guardian*, 2 August 2012.)

In my early years of bicycle commuting, I'd gone down seven times. Since then, my rides were 100% clean. Chalk it up to improved instincts or the statistical luck factor finally evening out after a dreadful run.

In a moment following a near miss with a truck, which should be called a near hit, I wrote an article challenging the Municipality of Paris. City leaders had encouraged the army of silent cyclists, I wrote, in order to democratize the streets and lower air pollution, but without providing us with enough infrastructure.

I hereby apologize to former Mayor Bertrand Delanoe and current Mayor Anne Hidalgo. The real culprit is still what Illich called the radical energy monopoly, the same types of companies that have lobbied against Parisian mayors' bicycle infrastructure policies every step of the way, trying to strip bike riders of their fair share of the streets.

WE NEED A NEW WORD FOR ENVIRONMENTALISM

In 2017, Madame Hidalgo began a ban on automobile traffic on the riverside "speedway" along the Seine River, a policy that would lead to law suits from the car lobby. Converting the banks of the Seine into a scenic gathering place was a copy of a revolutionary act famously applied in the USA in Portland, Oregon.

In 2018 I attended a community meeting at the Hotel de Ville (City Hall) to add my two cents, only to hear a car lobbyist affirm that the "smart car" was the answer to reducing pollution thanks to more efficient acceleration and breaking. At the end of 2018, Madame Hidalgo and other procycling mayors received an unexpected boost from the national government with its unprecedented Plan Velo, whose ambitious environmental target is to increase the proportion of employees nationwide commuting by bicycle from 3% to 9%. Critics to Hidalgo's riverfront plan trotted out environmental arguments themselves, claiming that eliminating a major route displaces the congestion to other streets, with resulting stop and go traffic contributing to even more air pollution. But six major freeway removals in recent history have shown that the creation of more public space has not added traffic jams. A theory called 'induced demand' proves that if you make streets bigger, more drivers will use them.

"When you make them smaller, drivers discover and use other routes, and traffic turns out to be about the same," according to Alissa Walker in "Six Free way Removals That Changed Their Cities Forever" (*Gizmodo* , 25 May 2016). To make her case she cites the removals of the Embarcadero Freeway in San Francisco; Cheonggyecheon in Seoul; Harbor Drive in Portland, Oregon; Park East, Milwaukee; Rio Madrid in Madrid; and Alaskan Way, Seattle. Each of these removals, she wrote, have improved urban quality of life in its own ways. The mayor of Paris doubled down on her critics with a bold idea: a year-long debating period, an exchange of ideas that might lead to free public transportation, including trains arriving from the suburbs, the main source of car commuter paralysis.

How many suburban drivers would be enticed by free public transportation to garage their cars and come to work by train, with or without a bike? Would healthcare savings coming from the cleaner air (reduced asthma and respiratory diseases) help pay for the transition? What are other ways to compensate for the lost revenue?

In fact we already have free public transportation, with our fares only paying for 27% of each ride, leaving our rides 73% free. In Paris, totally free public transport for gentrified residents might seduce cyclists to commute by metro, thereby further burdening an already congested system. These are things I learned from the City Hall debate.

Better to invest in making streets safer for bike riders and pedestrians. I look down from the stone railings of the early-17th-century Pont Neuf upon the liberated riverfront: lovers walking hand in hand, cyclists and skateboarders rolling freely and silently, old-timers sitting on benches reading Le Parisien, and I conclude that we need to change the word "environmentalism." We need a new word that makes it clear that protecting the air we breathe and water we drink is taking a stand for joie de vivre.

Too often the narrative of the fossil fuel lobbies associates the environmentalist with someone who wants to diminish your quality of life. The lobbyist has appropriated the word and poisoned it. Furthermore, even amidst chronic weather events that point to global warming, meteorologists, not wanting to be associated with environmentalists, shamelessly avoid the phrase climate change.

And anyway, who really wants to be labeled by a six-syllable word? The intrinsic problem with the word lies in the fact that its stressed syllable falls on a meaningless suffix: en-vi-ron-MENT-al-ist. What is a "ment"? Compare this to cli-mate-AC-ti-vist where the stress falls on a strong and meaningful syllable: Act. Activists against the Dakota Access Pipeline saw the linguistic trap and have called themselves "water protectors."

Through its own title, Friends of the Earth has found a more humane name recognition for reaching the public as the world's largest grassroots environmental network. Even the hugely influential climate activist group *350.org* does not use the E word when presenting its mission of keeping carbon in the ground, building a zero-carbon economy and pressuring governments into limiting emissions. There's never been a sitcom on environmentalism and British comedian Marcus Brigstocke has called climate change "far and away the most difficult comedy subject I've ever dealt with."

Lacking humorous outlets, some environmentalists fall into the unavoidable trap of sounding so grave that they seem conceited. I've gotten to know some of those solemn activists and have learned that they are usually remarkably humble, and not at all somber when talking about other subjects.

Too bad it took me decades to get over the altruistic gloominess of environmentalism. So let's change that word, cut out a few syllables, erase the "ment" and add something with more muscle, like act or resist, something that lets the public know it's a good fight.

A Stoic chimes in: virtue is sufficient for happiness

Back in my car driving days, an environmentalist quoted the Stoic Epictetus, telling me that virtue is sufficient for happiness and that I could do my commuting and vacationing on a bike to help the environment. He said that more than a quarter of all polluting gases come from motorized vehicles.

"Virtue seems like a good idea," I said, "but when it's associated with pedaling up steep hills under the hot sun, it takes the fun out of life." He was from the Midwest and didn't know about the hills. I had no clue about the untapped reserve of fuel in my own human tank.

An Epicurean gives it a try: The highest level of pleasure is the absence of pain.

Still during my car-driving era, a follower of Epicurus gave it a try. The highest level of pleasure, he said, is the absence of pain. Ride your bike to improve your health, lower your cholesterol, lower your blood pressure, strengthen the immune system, act as a deterrent against Alzheimer's and help yourself sleep better.

I looked out at the relentless and intimidating traffic whirring past our apartment on 12345 Burbank Boulevard in Van Nuys. Yes, I could reduce my cholesterol and boost my immune system but then get run over by a car, dying younger than if I'd became a couch potato. Thanks anyway, I told him, quoting Mark Twain: "Learn to ride a bicycle. You will not regret it if you live."

A Hedonist finally intervenes: Short-term pain, long-term pleasure

For years, Hedonists were too busy working hard at having fun to bother with my personal situation. But Guillaume, the bicycle philosopher who had "hired" me at the Vélorution outing, referred to the Hedonist, Aristippus, reminding me of how road cycling follows the contours of the land in a most sensual way.

My employer from the underground economy did warn me that Aristippus compared living according to pleasure to domesticating a horse. It often means choosing painful situations to get long term pleasure. Riding your bike up a steep hill may be a struggle. To enjoy it requires toughness, endurance. Hedonism is not for wimps. Pleasure requires virtue. You learn that virtue pays off splendidly when you cruise downhill after the climb.

Where was he when I needed his advice thirty years ago? Dozens of commutes and vacations devalued during my younger years when I believed that a bike was for sport only and not for travel.

In a world full of pain, pleasure should not be the target

Jean, my environmentalist-horseplayer friend loses the war of words by preaching that we should make sacrifices. A puritanical argument does not go well with his audience full of pleasure seekers who reside in a world full of pain. Self-interest works more effectively in most realms of life than sacrifice and altruism. When my wife and I dumped our cars and cut down our living space by 300 percent, we did so in order to eliminate the clutter that got in the way of true pleasure. No sacrifice!

When car and oil lobbyists condition our neurons into biophysical connections between pleasure and fossil fuel consumption, abstract environmental arguments about "crisis" and "urgency" are not visceral enough to disentangle those neurons. Only after the transition was complete and we were feeling a whole lot better, physically, psychologically, and financially, did she and I discover a neat fit between our happy liberation and the underlying philosophies of environmentalism.

In *Le Pouvoir de fa Pedale* (*The Power of the Pedal,* 2014), Olivier Razemon refers to a study of Copenhagen bicycle commuters:

> 56% chose the bike because it was fast;
> 37% responded that it was the practical solution;
> 29% said that cycling was saving them money;
> 26% claimed it was good for their health;
> 5% said they cycled for environmental reasons

Even though their motive is rarely the environment, their commuting on a bike correlates with better air quality. With more than 40% of its commutes by bike, the city of Copenhagen has significantly cleaner air than Paris, where less than 5% of commutes are by bike. Berlin's 15% bicycle modal share correlates with better air quality than Paris but not as clean as Copenhagen. (See: Copenhagen Account (2010): *Bicycle traffic in Copenhagen prevents 90,000 tons of CO2 from being emitted annually*)

Without considering other variables, these correlations do not prove in a causal sense that a higher percentage of bike commuters is the main reason for cleaner air. However, when a citizen decides to leave the car at home and take a bike instead, this one commute spews no toxicity into the air. Martha and I were not even aware of the concept of ecological footprint when we rid ourselves of so much excess baggage, so much stuff.

In his sketch, "Stuff," George Carlin notes that "your house is just a place for your stuff" ... "That's what your house is, a place to keep your stuff while you go out and get... more stuff!" He adds, "Have you noticed that their stuff is shit and your shit is stuff?"

With our three transformations:
> (a) cycling, walking or taking the train instead of driving;
> (b) purging our stuff and the space it occupied; and
> (c) drastically cutting consumption of red meat along with other industrially-produced foods, we had de-stuffed our lives.

Without the word "environmentalism," we had adopted a self-serving ecological lifestyle.

THE REBOUND EFFECT

Ministers of the Environment would have us believe that we can keep on consuming at the same level as long as wind, solar and other renewable energies reduce the environmental cost of such consumption. In the same way road engineers build wider roads to lower congestion only to see more cars rush into the added space, people look for larger houses to reduce clutter only to see more clutter fill their walk-in closets and bulging garages. "Sometimes you gotta move," said Carlin, "you gotta get a bigger house. Why? Too much stuff."

Or as civil engineer Charles Marohn explained: "Trying to solve congestion by making roadways wider is like trying to solve obesity by buying bigger pants."

One member of *The Guardian*'s environment desk admits to leaving his energy-saving light bulbs on more than traditional bulbs. Owners of fuel efficient cars tend to drive them more often. These are both examples of an often-overlooked phenomenon... the rebound effect. (Sylvia Rowley, "Could the rebound effect undermine climate efforts?" *The Guardian,* 22 Feb 2011.)

The rebound effect (aka Jevon's paradox) kicks in when technological progress increases the efficiency with which a resource is used only to trigger a rising use of that same resource. If the benefits of replacing fossil fuels with renewable energies were to be even partly nullified by increased consumption of the cleaner energy, then something else, something as simple as reducing consumption, would be needed to reduce CO_2 emissions and noxious pollution.

"Even if non-polluting power were feasible and abundant," wrote the visionary Illich back in the early 70s, "the use of energy on a massive scale acts on a society like a drug that is physically harmless but psychically enslaving."

The therapy machine

Of all the factors in the blissful downsizing in our household, the bicycle has played the most prominent role.

As a child in New York City I'd used my bike for daring urban races, with friends acting as human streetlights to stop cars from crossing our course during a race. It had not occurred to me that cycling was more than a sport until 45 years later when the City of Paris began promoting the bicycle as transportation.

As I began my bike commuting back in 2001, I was confronting ongoing family tragedies (eventually resolved by a pharmaceutical breakthrough and a gifted team of surgeons). During the seemingly endless tragedies, I would often wake up with zero motivation to get out of bed and go to a gig. But the bicycle was waiting for me.

As I wheeled toward my job of the day, my entangled spirit uncoiled. By the time I arrived at the gates of a school or the entrance hall of a company, my two-wheeled therapy machine had geared me up to make a positive impact on other people, some of whom were experiencing their own tragedies.

No therapist could have accomplished as much as my bicycle.

At this point it's worth mentioning that, following my adoption of regular bicycle commuting, my biannual blood tests (the French health care system saves money with such preventive measures) showed great improvements within all my potential danger categories. My cholesterol, for example, plunged from 200 to 170, with HD L and LDL moving in the right direction.

In 2017, *The British Medical Journal* published a University of Glasgow study of 264,337 participants which concluded that commuting by bike works significantly to cut the risk of developing cancer and cardiovascular disease.

"Cycling all or part of the way to work was associated with substantially lower risk of adverse health outcomes. Those who cycled the full length of their commute had an over 40 per cent lower risk of heart disease, cancer and overall mortality over the five years of follow-up," said Dr. Jason Gill of the Institute of Cardiovascular and Medical Sciences. (See: Jeffrey Stern, "New study says cycling 30 miles per week cuts heart disease and cancer risk in half," *Cycling Weekly*, 21 April 2017).

As George Carlin noted, the planet will be around long after we, as a species, are gone. Through legitimate self-interest, especially our personal health, a multitude of transformational activities, cycling being only one of them, might improve the odds for the survival of the human species and indirectly assure that the planet remains a livable place.

The Rebound Effect

Alternative or renewable energies will eventually replace fossil fuels. But as this happens, the Rebound Effect will kick in. Only by lowering consumption, downsizing or voluntary simplicity can we overcome the Rebound Effect. Most people are not going to make what they perceive to be sacrifices. But they will reduce consumption once they see and feel the magnificently therapeutic results of exorcising clutter and thriving on human energy.

CAN WE GO FASTER ON A BICYCLE THAN IN A CAR? *(With help from Ivan Illich)*

I had the honor, in the mid 1970s, to be among six people invited to share a round table conversation at the University of Illinois, Chicago with the great iconoclast, Ivan Illich, author of classic books like *Deschooling Society*. I could have arrived to this gathering by bicycle but I assumed that my car was faster.

Gross *speed vs. net speed*

In business, net income measures profits better than gross earnings before taxes and overhead are accounted for. Could net speed and gross speed exist as well? I ignored the distinction, perhaps because the education system Illich had excoriated had failed to emancipate my mind.

It would take 15 minutes by car from my apartment to the university where I worked. Add at least 5 minutes to find a parking space, to make it 20 minutes. The same distance by bike took 40 minutes, with immediate parking at my office building.

Had the transportation theme come up, Illich would have asked me how many work hours per week were dedicated exclusively to support my car. I'll answer him now, four decades later.

From the 40 hour work week I needed at least 8 hours (480 minutes) to earn enough for car expenses, which included the car itself, gas, oil changes, repairs, license, insurance, tires, wash, parking, tolls.

My 40-minute daily commutes by car equaled 200 minutes per week. To that amount Illich would add the 480 minutes of labor squandered to support the car. In sum I spent 680 minutes per week driving and working to pay car expenses. Conversely, if the bicycle were my means of transport, I'd need to work less than 50 minutes per week to cover minimal expenses: repairs, waterproof clothing for rainy days and the cost of the bike itself.

Net speeds summarized:

Car: 200 minutes driving/parking plus 480 minutes working to pay for car= 680 minutes spent

Bicycle: 400 minutes cycling plus 50 minutes working for bike expenses = 450 minutes spent

The bicycle was faster than the car because it consumed much less net time. Consider how Illich explained it in 1978. "The typical American male devotes more than 1600 hours a year to his car. He sits in it while it goes and while it stands idling. He parks it and searches for it. He earns the money to put down on it and to meet the monthly installments. He works to pay for gasoline, tolls, insurance, taxes, and tickets. He spends four of his sixteen waking hours on the road or gathering his resources for it."

"And this figure does not take into account the time consumed by other activities dictated by transport: time spent in hospitals, traffic courts, and garages. Time spent watching automobile commercials or attending consumer education meetings to improve the quality of the next buy. The model American puts in 1600 hours to get 7500 miles: less than five miles per hour, about half the speed of an urban cyclist." (The figures change according to the period but the concept remains identical.)

Illich's concept is applied to our contemporary period by Paul Tranter, using Google Maps and official statistics from transportation departments for painstaking calculations. For this, Tranter's credentials are impeccable: Ph. D, School of Physical, Environmental, and Mathematical Sciences, UNSW Canberra, Australia.

Tranter confirms Illich's theory in his articles "Effective Speed: Cycling Because It's Faster" and "Effective Speeds: Car Costs Are Slowing Us Down." Considering the costs of paying for, maintaining and parking a car, in function of hours worked, Tranter calculates the effective speed in dozens of cities around the world, including:

- New York: 10.6
- Los Angeles: 14.9
- Tokyo: 14.4
- London: 8.9
- Delhi: 8.0
- Nairobi: 3.1

The effective car speed km/h in all the cities he measures is slower than that of a bicycle.

The 14.9 for Los Angeles equals 9.25 m/p/h.

These effective speeds are reduced even more, Tranter believes, if we consider the external costs (CO_2 emissions pollution and the extra public health costs attributed to the more sedentary life associated with car dependency). This method for calculating effective speed seems reliable for compact cities like Paris, Barcelona, Amsterdam and Copenhagen, but somewhat less applicable to hopelessly sprawling North American cities, where the average commute seems too long to be practical. But in the last 15 years an infrastructure revolution has been changing the math. Transportation departments now house mobility offices, with "active transport" specialists who restore the rights of pedestrians and cyclists. Within the Complete Streets programs, motorized vehicles will no longer be the undisputed owners of urban space.

Of all the positive changes, perhaps the most transformational is the creation of bicycle space in expanding commuter train and metro networks, as well as bike racks on the front of buses. In Southern California, an employee who lives in Burbank or Anaheim can now arrive via Metrolink rail, with bicycle, to downtown LA, Union Station.

Blended transportation

Bicycle commuters can pedal to their station, park the bike and take the train. Or they can ride the bike to the station, take it comfortably into the train and get off at the station nearest their job, completing the trip on two wheels if necessary. Even with the Olympic distances of sprawling metropolitan areas, blended transportation effectively reduces cycling distance for the commuter.

Numerous municipalities in the USA have integrated their public transport with the bicycle, including New York, San Francisco, Seattle, Dallas, Pittsburgh and miraculously, Los Angeles, which had to begin from scratch.

But in applying Illich's and Tranter's effective speed method, the bicycle commuter who uses public transportation must add the cost of trains and buses to his work hours needed to finance the bicycle. Metrolink in LA, for example, is not cheap.

Some American employees have successfully negotiated for reimbursement of public transportation fares, which in most European countries are at least partially assumed by the employer. In France, cycling associations successfully lobbied for a law that enables companies to voluntarily reimburse the employee-cyclist according to number of kilometers of commuting.

To negotiate, bicycle commuters have two arguments:

(1) Their improved health thanks to cycling translates into higher productivity.

(2) If a person commuting 20 miles switches to transit, biking or walking, it reduces his or her carbon footprint by at least 4800 tons, equal to about 10 percent of all greenhouse emissions in a typical two-adult, two-car household. (See Jay Walljasper: "11 reasons why trains, buses, bikes and walking move us toward a brighter future," PBS Project for Public Spaces, 28 January 2015.)

The cost of public transportation is still minimal compared to what's required to support a car. And less tangible savings for the cyclist exist. Consider the cost of fitness clubs, almost a necessity for commuters who are immobilized for so many hours in their cars. Doctors Ornstein and Sobel write that if an employee were to cycle to work, he would no longer have to pay for the health club. They explain with data that purposeful physical activity contributes more to health than forced exercise (*HealthyPleasures*, "Why Kill Yourself to Save Your Life," p 103).

With the monthly savings from dodging the fitness club, the bicycle commuter can pay for public transportation. However, blended transportation does not fully resolve the challenge of sprawling cities. Los Angeles has only 8,000 inhabitants per square mile, compared to 27,000 for New York. Without useful density, commuting distances expand while dead space ("non-places") accumulate. Paris has 55,000 inhabitants per square mile, Barcelona 40,000. It's no surprise that getting around in these cities is easier and more aesthetically pleasing than in urban sprawl.

On hot days in compact cities with buildings close to streets, the cyclist glides through pleasant shady reprieves. But in more expansive cities it is rare to find buildings lining streets. Made for the car, the "city of the angels" has allowed the devil to insert vast parking lots between sidewalks and commerce. Buildings fail to provide shade for pedestrians or cyclists on scorching afternoons. And the sensorial deprivation: a massive 14% of Los Angeles County surface area is occupied by parking lots!

To defend already excessive rental values, LA real estate interests leverage to prevent new housing that would increase density. "There is a well-established correlation between higher-density neighborhoods and the feasibility of cycling," wrote Carol Feucht of the LA County Bicycle Coalition (*LATimes*, 6 March 2017). "The farther people are from work, the more likely they are to drive." If Illich and Tranter recalculated car speed based on the insanely congested LA freeways, effective speed would plummet. Ironically, lack of density can contribute to greater congestion because it forces more people on to the freeway, and for longer distances.

Los Angeles has joined the worldwide movement that embraces cycling to reduce congestion and improve public health. But lack of density remains a major obstacle. Influenced by this urban revolution, various cities less apt for cycling as transport are nevertheless joining the trend. For example, Brisbane, Australia, one of the most car dependent places on earth, with only 896 souls per square mile, has established an extraordinary bicycle infrastructure with every imaginable facility. Singapore, extremely car-dependent, whose new "Car Lite" program seeks to drastically reduce the number of automobiles, has redefined the bike as a mode of transport.

Singapore eliminated chewing gum from the streets. Will it also eliminate cars?

Mountainous La Paz, Bolivia (12,000 feet altitude) has taken blended transport to a new level, literally, allowing bikes to board the cabins of the Teleférico aerial cable car transport system. Who is responsible for this transformation in urban culture? In the mid-twentieth century, the oil and car lobbies got municipalities to uproot their rail transport (LA) or refrain from building a metro train system (Detroit). Today bike, pedestrian and public transport associations have reversed the trend, but not without opposition. In 2011, the former mayor of Toronto, Rob Ford, announced the removal of the bike-way from one of the two main Toronto arteries, declaring that the battle against cars was over.

In 2013 the Wall Street Journal lamented the influence of the totalitarian "bike lobby," declaring that New York has never suffered a threat so severe as the BikeShare program. In New York, between 2007 an 2013, during the pro-cycling administration of Janette Sadik-Kahn (Transport Department Commissioner), people referred to "the traffic war." In her "The Bike Wars Are Over and the Bikes Won" (NY Magazine, 8 March, 2016), Sadik Kahn gives credit to numerous activist organizations, such as Transportation Alternatives, for the victory of the cyclists, pedestrians and public transport users.

An emblematic event from the period revealed a Critical Mass cyclist brutally assaulted by a police officer, viral on Youtube . Critical Mass groups vary from those that occupy streets to gain urban space, such as Vélorution in Paris, to others that operate in coordination with municipal authorities, such as the Miami group, which may even get a police escort. Throughout North America, hundreds of associations, less extravagant than Critical Mass, advocate with increasing success in favor of cycling as transport, including the one I belong to, MDB (Mieux se Déplacer à Bicyclette).

According to Salvador Fuentes Bayó, Environmental Services Manager from Barcelona, "the role of the associations in promoting the bicycle has been fundamental." As is often the case, the ideas of visionaries are often put into practice after they've died. Ivan Illich is not here to see his ideas moving forward successfully, ahead of the traffic.

(Some of the material in this chapter originally appeared in Suburbano.net, and in Cycling Industry News)

FROM TRUCK FARMING TO BIKE FARMING

For an egg to arrive in our kitchen it has to make several trips. From the farm it travels by truck to a wholesaler. From the wholesaler it hitches another truck ride to the supermarket. And in automobile cultures it gets picked up at the market and taken by car to the consumer's home. You can't see it but the egg is bathed in oil.

Sometimes the egg doesn't rest between trips and gets to the supermarket within two days but the best-case scenario is 72 hours, and sometimes an egg takes as long as a month to make it to our kitchen. The voyage of a tomato is longer. The study "Food, Fuel and Freeways" (*ngfn.org*, June 2001) concluded that the average tomato traveled 1,369 miles to arrive at the Terminal Market in Chicago, where wholesalers sell to supermarkets and restaurants. After a rest at the wholesale market, the tomato still had two more trips in order to arrive at our kitchen.

When we sit down today to dine, instead of the Lord's Prayer we hear the lamentation, "Tomatoes don't taste like they used to." This lack of flavor "is the collateral effect of the need for commercial qualities in the tomato," explains researcher Antonio Granell with unintended irony.

Urban agriculture

Among the various methods to eliminate farming's dependency on fossil fuels is urban agriculture. I tried peri-urban agriculture for a year and a half, back in the early 80s, before it became the rage. It was fun and I learned a few things about where my food comes from, but I lacked the foresight to connect my work to the farmers markets that were beginning to make an impact in Los Angeles. It did not occur to me that produce could be transported by bicycle to the farmers' market and I used a car for deliveries to Korean markets.

My mistakes aside, I was able to establish a food recycling system whereby I picked up leftovers from local restaurants in 5-gallon tins and gave this unused food a second chance with my pigs and hens. Who knows, perhaps today environmentalists might find a flaw in my innovation. In any case, my experiment with peri-urban and urban agriculture came too soon and with too little foresight, so I now defer to far better models in which the bicycle plays a central role in urban agriculture.

Today savvy urban farmers are using bicycle power to deliver their produce to local farmers' markets. Urban agriculture is in a boom period in scattered areas of North and South America, and Europe, following advances coming from Asia. The most dramatic examples seem to emerge when people's backs are to the wall during periods of crisis, as with Havana in the 1990s (which I witnessed and covered as a reporter) and devastated areas of bankrupt Detroit, Michigan today.

Rising Pheasant Farms is an important producer of vibrant community-commercial agriculture in a place where it is most needed. In 2014 alone they produced nearly 180,000 kg of food within more than 1,300 community plots on family or commercial property in Detroit.

With her husband, Carolyn Leadley operates Rising Pheasant Farms. "The peas that travel only 5 km to give life to a salad are undoubtedly tastier and more nutritious than those that travel half a continent or even farther," Leadley said. (See: *globalvoices.org*, 24 June 2015). On *YouTube* you can see videos of the Leadleys transporting their produce to market by bicycle (*www.youtube.com/watch?vfv2mAKCHTMs*)

In Orlando, Florida we learn how "Bike-Powered Farming Program Turns Lawns Into Urban Farms" (*EcoWatch*, 22 May 2016). "Fleet Farming, a bike-powered, all-volunteer team of farmers in Orlando, Florida is turning wasteful, water-hogging lawns into mini urban farms to help boost local food production. Here's how it works. A landowner or renter with owner consent, can donate their chemical-free lawn to Fleet Farming. Once the site is assessed and approved for growing, Fleet Farms will schedule the installation of a food-producing plot at least 500 square feet in size."

Farmers use bikes to pedal from one home plot to another to plant and harvest the produce. What's grown at the yard gardens is then sold at local farmers markets and restaurants within a five-mile bikeable radius. Then there's Chain Reaction Urban Farm (see *Ethical-Foods.com*), where a small urban farm in Saskatoon delivers fresh organic produce to the neighbors by bicycle. The farm is run by former urban educators Jared Regier and his wife Rachel. As in the Orlando program, the Regiers use borrowed backyards within the city.

Throughout North America, public associations or private sector enterprises are following a similar model, such as the coop, Cycle Alimen Terre, Montreal, which produces and distributes healthy, fresh and hyper-local greens. We learn from the group's website that, "All of our seeds and materials are organic and our distribution is done by bicycles."

Dozens of bicycle-powered urban agriculture projects are located strategically in food deserts. The USDA defines food desert as parts of the country lacking fresh fruit, vegetables and other healthful whole foods, usually found in impoverished areas, largely due to lack of food providers such as groceries, farmers' markets and health food stores. A USDA map shows the largest number of US food deserts in southern states, once known as agricultural regions.

In such food deserts, replacing wholesome food suppliers are local quickie marts and even liquor stores that "provide a wealth of processed sugar and fat-laden foods that are known contributors to our nation's obesity epidemic."

The Food and Agriculture Organization of the United Nations (FAO) encourages and provides technical support for urban agriculture projects in the developing world. "It is estimated that garden plots can be up to 15 times more productive than rural holdings. An area of just one square meter can provide 20 kg of food a year."

"The intensive cultivation of a wide range of vegetables, roots and tubers, and herbs in small spaces, known as micro-gardening, is sustainable and highly productive and can be easily managed by anyone." (See: *www.fao.org/ soils 2015/news/news detail/en/c/329009*)

"I have seen the future, and the future is bicycles."

Agriculture economist William Grisley reminds us that using bicycles for farming is nothing new in Asia. "The importance of bicycles to agriculture and rural development is well-known in many Asian countries. Bicycles have long been a familiar part of the landscape, and are the primary means of transport for agricultural inputs and outputs for many small-scale farmers" (see "I have seen the future and the future is bicycles," published by *The FAO*, 1995.)

With years of experience in Africa, Grisley tells us that the bicycle is now making inroads in sub-Saharan agriculture. He refers specifically to Uganda, the East African country "where the importance of bicycles as a means of transport for small-scale farmers is increasing dramatically. Bikes now dominate in the transportation of agricultural commodities produced within a 35-kilometre radius of selected retail markets around the capital city of Kampala."

With an increasing portion of the world's population living in or migrating to urban and peri-urban areas, local urban agriculture makes more sense than ever. The bicycle is playing an increasing role in localizing agriculture and thus eliminating fossil fuels from production and distribution of good food.

(Some of the material in this chapter originally appeared in Suburbano.net and in Systemic Alternatives.)

MISSION BOLIVIA

The bicycle philosopher had sent me on a mission: to prove that bicycle commuting was possible in "any city in the world!" That's what he said. But he'd never seen La Paz, Bolivia. I had no trouble with Paris and Barcelona, and even Los Angeles, California was getting easier with added bike lanes and the blending of bicycle routes with public transportation such as bike racks on buses and bike-cars in the Metrolink commuter trains.

LaPaz, Bolivia, however, was an extreme test. The altitude alone, with drastic ups and downs ranging between 11,000 and 13,000 feet above sea level, was intimidating, to say the least. At that altitude one breathes in only 60% as much oxygen as the amount in a breath of air at sea level!

Good things about living in thin air

Yes, breathing is not easy in La Paz, but there are advantages of living at extreme altitudes. A few examples:

- You can leave a cut-open avocado on the kitchen table in the morning and it will still be green for dinner time. At a normal altitude, avocado flesh rots when exposed to oxygen, turning it an unappealing brown color. Not here.

- Home owners don't need to buy fire insurance. Not enough oxygen to start or sustain a fire. Pyromaniacs flee from La Paz to lower altitudes.

- Most of the world's most successful animals, insects, cannot survive in the rare air. This includes the most dangerous animal of all, the mosquito. In my five years living in La Paz, I was not bitten once by a mosquito.

In exchange for a life without mosquitoes, it's worth having to learn all over again how to breathe, and then how to cycle without getting wiped out. Even over flat terrain, cycling at this literally breathtaking altitude would be a terrifying enterprise. But it gets more frightening. In La Paz, none of the very few flat streets lead anywhere, as they are mainly cross streets. Most of the important routes have gradients that would qualify as Class 2 and Class 1 climbs in the Tour de France!

This city is squeezed into a "hole" in the ground, with canyons slashing every which way through the mountains, which means there is little space for motorized transport. Bus and car traffic faces gridlock hot spots in various bottlenecks around the city. No amount of classic transportation planning can overcome such geographic determinism.

As of 2014, age 69, we had decided to spend six weeks of every year in La Paz, our former home during the second half of the 1990s. As the plane landed at El Alto Airport, I compared myself to an independent astronaut on a maiden mission but with no NASA controllers to guide me. From the high-plain airport, the sight of the white-robed Cordillera Real seduced me into re-living my hiking experiences of the 1990s. But looking down into the gaping urban fissures, I had serious doubts about getting more than two or three blocks on a bike. Even in Paris I was a slowpoke in biking up a hill, and that was near sea level.

After three days of rest in order to reacclimate to the altitude, I began some serious hiking to prepare myself for eventual cycling. Following the week of hiking, a mild flu thwarted my cycling plans for another 10 days. The hiking-to-acclimate strategy was a serious tactical mistake. I should have started cycling from the get-go. Now I was already three weeks into my six-week stay.

One Sunday morning, out to buy some crusty marraqueta bread for breakfast, I came across a group of sleekly-uniformed cyclists preparing for an outing. I asked if they knew of any used bike for sale.

"Why don't you try this one while we wait for our friends," said a future Nairo Quintana, in an Argentine accent. "It's an Italian bike. I work for a bike shop in Obrajes and this is my second bike." The bike's gear shifting system was weird but solid. I got on, went easily over two flat blocks and then turned right, up a hill. To my surprise the uphill was invigorating, at least for the first block. As I continued the climb, I felt a need for an oxygen mask. The gradient was steeper than my favorite hills in the Montmorency Forest near Paris.

Rolling back downhill was a mini-pleasure with a maxi-message for the future. This can be done. Thanks to the quick test on the Italian bike, I persuaded myself that I was not giving up! Back at the apartment, I did some serious thinking. Given the shortness of breath I'd felt over the second block of my climb, in order to do this right, I would need an entire six-week stay in La Paz for a truly incremental adaptation to cycling the unavoidable hills. I had only three weeks left. The thin wheels on the Italian racing bike were not appropriate for the rough terrain ahead of me and even if I tried to get going immediately, I would lose another day or two combing the city for the right bicycle. Of course these arguments may have been my rationalizing as a result of the intimidating geography.

I resolved to view my goal in the long term, continue my hiking expeditions for the rest of my stay, and once back to France, do some serious hill cycling to train for the next annual stay in La Paz, at which time I would purchase a bike upon arrival. One thing for sure. Some of the glaciers I'd gotten to know and learned to love back in 1998-99 had disappeared, with potentially dire consequences for the city's water supply. This was my first eye-witness view of the results of global warming. All the more reason to prove that cycling on human energy can begin to replace motorized transport in any city in the world, even La Paz!

LegalEPO

My planned strategy would reverse what I knew about human biology: it would require that I become stronger as I got older. This first renewal of my residence in La Paz taught me a lesson. Before I'd left France, my red blood cell count had been near the anemia level. Upon returning, I took another blood test. Thanks to the hiking at high altitudes, my blood scores registered healthy effects so substantial that they were comparable to EPO...but an entirely legal form of doping.

Such strength and stamina were so notable that, once back near sea level, I confused the doping effects with rejuvenation. Whatever, it was the right time to add thousands of kilometers in bicycle touring, with climbing as well as expanded distances as integral parts of my itineraries! Concentrating on the present, but without micro-managing my upcoming bicycle travels, I'd be preparing myself to take on La Paz, Bolivia on two wheels.

Arriving in Paris my subconscious, in successive currents of jet-lagged dreams, forced me to look back on the stay in La Paz. I heard myself being called spineless, chicken, indecisive, wimp, tentative, wussy, namby-pamby and pushover. No amount of rationalization could have excused my failure to have started cycling in La Paz from the get-go.

Shaking off my humiliation, I was as determined as ever to prove that even a non-athletic old man can do regular cycling in the most impossible settings. Getting around on two wheels in La Paz had become my personal Everest.

II.
BICYCLE TOURING

BICYCLE TOURING VS. BICYCLE ENDURING

A basic definition of bicycle touring is bike travel with a minimum of one overnight stay. No maximum: you can cycle from Alaska to Ushuaia or take a trans-Asia route through all the countries that end in "...istan" if you choose. Or, you can discover places ignored by tour guides not that far from your own home. I see two types of bike touring: (A) where you endure the maximum to prove a point, or (B) where you use a sufficient amount of human energy to revel in rolling on the road.

I once attended a slide presentation in a funky café by a woman who had cycled for a year and a half across Asia. When listeners learned that she did not even get flat tires and that the creepiest foods did not compel her to stagger into an emergency room, they fidgeted, seemingly ready to get up and leave. But when she mentioned being threatened with rape by a guy in one of the -istan countries, they got into it. When they learned that the guy was a police officer, the enchantment intensified.

To their credit, they were still relieved to hear how the woman had talked her way out of it. Here was a lesson if you're planning a slide show of your vacation. If everything went just fine and there were no fuck-ups, most people don't want to see your pictures! This is why so many *Youtube* bike trekkers reassure us that they embarked on their trip knowing nothing about bicycle touring and learning by trial and error. They know that the primeval thrill of most audiences involves survival from misfortune, The best way to define bicycle touring is an example of what it is not.

In the BBC documentary, *The Man Who Cycled the Americas*, superman Mark Beaumont spends four one-hour episodes mainly huffing and puffing, seemingly in need of a transfusion. He is cycling the length of the longest mountain range on earth, the Rockies and the Andes. But his 13,000 mile itinerary avoids some of the most eye-catching and culturally stimulating places. The "length of the Andes" does not mean "through" them, and his route avoids most of the Cordilleras, preferring the low-lying coastal desert route instead. He misses places like Macchu Picchu and Lake Titicaca, while he circumvents Colombia, gateway to the Andes, depriving us of a glimpse of the second most biologically diverse country in the world.

Beaumont must have breezed through Costa Rica in a blink of the eye because the viewer does not catch a single frame of the only nation in the world without a standing army, once ranked first among 140 countries by the Happy Planet Index (HPI). (HPI considers four factors: ecological footprint, well-being, life expectancy and inequality.)

I had plenty of reasons to sing *Let's Call the Whole Thing Off.* Instead I composed an instant song called *Bet It or Regret It,* and was on my way. I call this bicycle touring, or enduring. Bike touring should not be reserved for the exclusive club of extreme sport survivalists. I present myself as an example: not endowed athletically, beset with health issues typical of one in his mid-70s and overwhelmed by family commitments, I have all the excuses needed to keep me from taking to the road.

Does this mean that non-athletes should give up on the extreme-sport edge of bicycle touring? Not really. Let's admire the record breakers like Mark Beaumont, so that on certain splendid mornings with an open road before us, we can rejoice in testing our strength and endurance, climbing 4 percent gradients and whizzing through beaux villages with not a moment to stop and gawk, in order to cover 120 kilometers before the sun sets.

Small extremes

Without hopelessly competing against others, I can compete against my own limitations, in what I call the joy of small extremes. Yes, sometimes I purposely choose the road with the toughest climbs. But above all, I'm proud to specialize in finding the most comfortable routes, thereby proving that bike touring is possible for a majority of members of my species.

So exactly what is bicycle touring?

Catalyzed by my bicycle mentor from Vélorution, nurtured by the thoughts of Ivan Illich, and learning from bike companions like Alan and Philippe and my wife Martha, I've come up with three guidelines:

1. Bicycle touring is slower than a motor trip, thus closer to the contour of the land and more drawn into the surrounding ways of life.

2. It's based on experience more than sightseeing. (But you can stop at any time and contemplate the view.) This experience is an exquisite blend of sport and geography, absolutely unrelated to either a sedentary bus tour or indoor cycling laps.

3. It uses the cheapest and most renewable source of energy, human energy, aided by the most energy-efficient form of transportation, the bicycle.

Even after bike commuting had become second nature, dozens of "what-if" factors deterred me from bike touring:

*   What if I ran out of human "gas" in the middle of nowhere?
*   What if the sun was setting and there was no lodging within range?
*   What if the bike broke down by a remote corn field with the needed repair more complicated than replacing an inner tube?
*   What if I ran out of a medication related to my ten nagging health conditions?
*   What if a savage heat wave arrived on the day when my trip was to begin?
*   What if I got lost?

TRIAL AND ERROR

Technical advances in transportation, for example the jumbo jet and the high-speed train, are the product of years of incremental improvements, with no quick transition from A to Z. I found myself at the A of bicycle touring. If I'd been young, I could do each step of the sequence in its appropriate time. But after discovering that my own mortality might arrive before I got to F or G, I decided to compress the bike touring process into abbreviated stages.

1. Begin by discovering the best ways to get out of Paris; NE: Canal de l'Ourcq; E: Bords de La Marne; S: Coulée Verte, and N: skirting the Forêt de Montmorency; each escape involving at least an hour and a half of cycling to reach the countryside.

2. Lift the bike into a commuter train until past the suburbs, then do day trips in the countryside. I did as much as 5 hours on a single trip. (In LA I could accomplish the same by using the comfortable bicycle car of a Metrolink train.)

3. Now ready for overnight trips, comb through contour maps to identify relatively flat trips that would delight my wife Martha. She's the more athletic half of our team of two, but she's discouraged by three things: prolonged climbs, urban traffic and the sun in her face.

4. Begin serious climbing in France, with my Bolivia mission in mind, increasing the number of uphill meters but also improving the ease with which I climbed.

5. Do more extended overnight journeys with younger friends, testing my strength and stamina.

6. Buy a bike in La Paz, Bolivia and begin cycling there.

7. Take a long bike trip and just keep going …

I considered the bike-touring menu.

Organized trips with a specialized company. A pick-up truck carries your travel possessions to the next stop. You give up self-determination but in return you get like-minded world citizens as companions. You don't have to scout for a hotel or campground or figure out how and when to eat along the way. Organized trips are expensive but the service is of great value.

Travel Light: Just carry a change of clothing, picnic food, water, sunblock and for old-timers, whatever meds you need. Pass through towns where food, lodging and even bike repairs can be found, keeping near train lines in case a breakdown (human or bike) requires transportation to a doctor or repair shop. Minimize the cost by buying food in supermarkets and stay in local family-run hotels, inexpensive gîtes, or even for free with the *warmshowers.org* network.

Self-sufficient travel: with panniers to carry water, food, clothing, repair tools, a tent and even electronic equipment, to be recharged at a campground. In exchange for the independence, you get to carry a heavy load. (See: *bicycletouringpro.com*) For our first trip, Martha and I decided on the travel-light option. After so much preparation, we still hesitated.

Arguments for not going

Martha is particularly sensitive to the sun. I needed an advanced degree in Avoid-the-Sun-in-the-Face Long-Distance Cycling. My thesis: calculate the angle of the sun throughout the journey, and time it so we'd be rolling through shielding forests at the most sun-drenched times of day. I had to avoid the longer steeper climbs that Martha was not accustomed to, and to assure her we'd find a place to sleep in non-tourist towns not famous for an abundance of lodging. Too many things could go wrong. A heat wave loomed in the weather forecasts and neither of us handles the heat.

Arguments for going

I had discovered the easy-rolling serenity of French "departmental routes," those secondary "D roads," with sparse traffic which follow the contour of the land. In the end, I'd done my homework. No excuse for putting it off any longer.

The plan

Day 1: a summer Saturday would see us traveling out of Melun (just past south Paris suburbs) to Rozay-en-Brie. I calculated that we'd pass through a forest during the mid-afternoon sun-and-heat period and rejoiced that the sun would be at our backs past noon as we were going east-north-east. Stay at a hotel in the beau village of Rozay-en-Brie.

Day 2: we would reach the splendid medieval fortress city of Provins on Sunday, taking the train back to Paris that night. Each day would cover more than 40 kilometers, sight-seeing detours included: certainly a modest goal for our first-ever bike tour.

Gallant knight with bike as steed

Saturday went perfectly. We saw two castles: the baroque Vaux-le-Vicomte (a Versailles on a more human scale) and the medieval Chateau de Blandy-les-Tours (centuries XIII to XIV) with its five imposing towers, with time to tour the stony interior of Blandy and picnic in the castle gardens. Perfect timing: the forest ride came up precisely during the hottest part of the afternoon. The last leg in late afternoon was freshened with iridescent rolling green hills.

The mild climb into colorful Rozay was energizing. Rozay was the type of classic French town you'd see in Readers Digest. A French Norman Rockwell would have painted Rozay. We found a basic but comfortable hotel. I was proud of myself, for having protected my wife from travel stress. I was a gallant knight with a bike as my steed. Everything that went right on the first day was destined to go wrong on Day 2.

On Sunday the heat wave plodded in at full force. The heavy humid heat was less oppressive in the morning but our east-south-east direction to Provins meant we'd have the direct sun in our faces until about 1:00 pm. If we waited, we'd have the sun only glancing us from the side; however, it would be hotter. Both options were bad decisions.

We decided to wait and hope for an afternoon breeze. Of course, hope cannot pass for a strategy. To get a feel for Rozay, my wife went to Mass (a rare event for her) and I hung out in the shade on the main square, watching our bikes and chatting with Sunday strollers. As the only stranger in church Martha won an extended chat with the local priest.

The first third of our trip out of Rozay went smoothly enough, and I expected that our arrival at route D 231 would be a straight shot to Provins.

The Road (with thanks to Cormac McCarthy)

But in my years of day trips, I'd never encountered a D road with such heavy traffic, mainly massive tornado-generating trucks. With each passing semi we had to pull over onto the thin shoulder, hoping to not get blown into the roadside ditch.

Lesson 1: Beware of straight roads. They are magnets for oppressive traffic.

The afternoon sun was pounding against my right cheek, a furnace-like headwind blew in the face and the 32 Celsius temperature was rapidly depleting us. Martha's attendance at mass had failed to win us a smoother trip, even with direct intervention from the priest.

The surface of the road was coarse gravel, with the resulting heavy friction turning mild climbs into torture sessions. Resolution: never again diatribe against the stationary bike in an air-conditioned fitness club.

We stopped along the road. I unfolded my map, which told me that the winding side roads in the nearby hills would double our distance, so I insisted, stupidly, on staying on D231.

Lesson 2: It's often better (and even faster) to double the distance on more comfortable roads.

We reached an intersection near a few stray houses and we both collapsed in a shady patch of pasture, luckily avoiding the cow dung. A farmer's wife came out of a house with a pitcher of cold water. We filled up our bottles. She pointed up into the nearby hills. "Ride up there and just make a right at the first intersection. It will take you into Provins. You'll love the road. You NEVER should have taken D231."

I recalled Cormac McCarthy's dystopian novel, *The Road,* in which father and son stick to the dangerous main road, expecting security there from marauders, only to discover near the end of the story that it would have been far safer to avoid "The Road."

When longer is easier

The shady climb into the hills led to a meandering road providing enough tree cover along the way to protect us from the evil sun. "Unforgettable" is an understatement for this is cycling lesson in motion: longer is often easier. We made it to Provins, walking the bikes up a steep and narrow street to the medieval city.

We needed three or four hours to really enjoy the town but thanks to *my* egregious mapping mistakes, we only had time for a refreshing ice cream and a quick walking tour around the castle-fortress. I had promises to keep on Monday or we'd have stayed overnight.

The morale of the story: it's possible to meticulously plan a bicycle tour and still make dumb mistakes. This was my maiden bike tour. I've never been one to do something right on the first try and the trip to Provins confirmed this character flaw.

I repeated my lessons: the longer route is often the easier one and avoid the straightest roads.

PRACTICING TO BECOME A BIKE GUIDE
WITH A DEMANDING TOURIST

Here was my chance to make amends for the near disastrous second day of the overnight bike tour to Provins: a five-day, four-night trip through the Loire chateau country: the type of vacation we used to take by car. Learning from previous bad decisions, I over-planned, in search of perfection. I only had one demanding customer: my wife.

- Find routes that avoided the sun, or placed the sun behind us.
- Minimize climbs. The Loire river route is flat but without tree cover, so I needed to map out routes through forests, with a few benign hills.
- Keep distances short enough so we'd have enough time to visit at least three castles.
- Avoid roads with noxious vehicle traffic.
- Find overnight stays with bike facilities.

Our bikes could handle both road travel and dirt paths, wheels not too wide, not too thin. Using maps from *The Institut Géographique National (IGN)* and the regional tourist office: *france.tourisme.chambordcountry.com*, I marked out an itinerary. Choosing routes is a fundamental joy of bicycle touring.

Day 1: cycle to the Austerlitz station and, bike-in-train, arrive at Beaugency on the Loire. Visit the medieval Beaugency castle, then cycle across the river to an inexpensive family-run hotel in Lailly, the gateway to signposted forest dirt-bike paths that would lead us to more castles: 15 km.

Day 2: stock up on picnic food at a ma-and-pa *épicerie*, cycle through the forest some 35 kilometers to Bracieux, the village nearest to the immense and flamboyant renaissance Chateau de Chambord. Stay two nights at Hotel La Bonnheure, whose owner, a cyclist himself, is available for tips and has bike maintenance facilities.

Day 3: visit the Chambord castle and explore other forest cycling paths: 25 kilometers minimum. (According to the Blois-Chambord public relations office, in 2016 more than 500 bicycles per day passed through the mythic *Chateaux à vélo* paths.)

Day 4: cycle to Blois, 25 km, leave bikes at another family-owned hotel, visit the Blois Castle and its 75 spiraling staircases, where Joan of Arc went in 1429 to be blessed by the archbishop before departing with her army. Tour the multi-leveled riverfront city of Blois, which seems to have existed since the 6th century, then see the *son-et-lumière* show in the castle at sundown.

Day 5: take the train to Paris. Cycle back home from the Austerlitz station: 10 km. This would be Martha's first 100+ kilometer bike trip, a total of 110 km. With such over-planning, not much room was left for the unexpected. But unforeseen events intervened nonetheless.

- In the forest between Lailly and Bracieux we dealt with up-hill segments where Martha discovered that climbing could become pleasant in a car-free shady context.

- Also between Lailly and Bracieux, with no comfortable place for our picnic lunch, we requested permission to use a bench on a private farm. Not only did we get the okay but the jolly woman brought us some fresh tomatoes, just harvested. Ever since, I've been searching, in vain for tomatoes with such an intense flavor.

- Between Bracieux and Blois we made a wrong turn and ended up on a prettier farm route with an expansive view of rural France.

- On the train from Blois to Paris, we realized we'd forgotten to stamp our tickets. Before the controllers arrived to hand us a stiff fine, we got off at Meung sur Loire, to stamp our tickets and wait for the next train. But once off the train, we decided to bike down into the beautifully preserved beau village of Meung and visited its 12th century castle. This was a stop we should have planned.

So before I pat myself on the back for a successful debut as a bicycle tour guide, I should admit: some of the most memorable moments of the tour were precisely what I had NOT planned for, and only thanks to a dumb mistake were we able to visit a fourth castle.

Government planning had set the table for my own micro-plan, thanks to the Regional Tourism Committee. Within the Blois-Chambord area alone, their infrastructure includes more than 400 kilometers of secure and marked cycling paths as well as bucolic farm roads permitting motor vehicles but marked with signs giving cyclists and horses the right of way.

One of the stated missions of these local authorities is to accompany the ecological transformation of tourism, in support of soft traffic, notably bicycles and horses. Pampered by a perfect setting, I'd had it easy proving to Martha that, Sí se puede!... she was now my co-conspirator.

Haiku adventures

I needed her moral support. I was about to take on a more daunting tour, and without her: from Paris to the sea. Nothing that Darren Alff, the Bicycle Touring Pro, would video home about, but a big deal for one who was just learning the ropes.

The trip would require cycling more than 100 kilometers on the first day, during a heat wave, and using a knobby-tired mountain bike, since my touring bike had been stolen on the eve of this trip, which I'd planned with my friend Philippe.

If a Bicycle Touring Pro cycling odyssey across an entire continent is equivalent to an epic poem, then my attempt at making it from Paris to the sea would be a humble 17 syllables in the scheme of things.

FROM PARIS TO THE SEA

It once took me four months to translate a haiku poem by the Mexican poet José Juan Tablada into English. I wasted two months trying to conform to the 17-syllable rule, until the editor told me that the "rule" is based on something that makes sense in Japanese, not so much in English. Finally I settled for 14 syllables and the translation was published.

This is another way of saying that my cycling trip from Paris to the sea figured to be more difficult than it seemed. On my maps of France, I could see the English Channel beaches only inches away from Paris! The more I unfolded my Cartes IGN (*Institut Géographique National*) and highlighted potential routes, the more I got into it viscerally.

My friend Philippe, a computer engineer and progressive activist, was overly impressed that I'd pulled off modest bike trips with Martha. "Let's do it!" he said. Our target was the harbor and beach city of Dieppe. Having seen his battered racing bike, I'd assumed that Philippe had experience with such adventures. But in fact, we were like two student pilots ready to do our first landing, each thinking that the other was the instructor.

Off the tourist circuit, Dieppe hyped its history museum in a medieval fortress on a huge bluff overlooking La Manche (The Channel). Dieppe was home to a working class stevedore culture with ma-and-pa bistros in industrial neighborhoods that Anthony Bourdain would have visited. Dieppe's beach spread out beneath the palisades, albeit strewn with ankle-spraining stones. It was the Contre-Riviera. I spread the map out on Philippe's oak dining room table, outlining a 120 plus kilometer trip from Gisors to Dieppe, the second half of which was all voie verte, a car-free bike-pedestrian "boulevard." I reminded myself that this was going to be my first 100+ kilometer day, a major portion of the Avenue Verte Paris-London.

For dramatic effect, I'll pronounce my plan in one elongated sentence, holding my breath. We'd take the train past the suburbs, get out at Gisors, ride the bending departmental roads through farmland and forests, reach the Voie Verte in the farming spa town Forges-les-Eaux, which dated back to the Romans, roll down to Dieppe before sundown, take in the sea at sunset, dine in a working class café, dump our backpacks in a cheap hotel, and the next morning cycle up and down the coast, along the palisades, scaling demanding bluffs and then swooping into a cove to enjoy the day's catch in a seafood bistro. We could return to Paris by train, late afternoon from the Dieppe station. But two obstacles, one from nature and the other manufactured, threatened to derail our arrival in Dieppe.

Silent predator

In the days leading up to our early-July trip, temperatures were in the low and mid-seventies, the humane norm for Paris. But forecasts called for a two day spike in temperatures, precisely at the time of our trip. Forget world climate trends, this heat wave was targeting me, personally: my silent predator.

We got off the train at Gisors just before 10am and began riding in a sweet breeze over undulating rural roads. By 11am, once out of the forest, we were taking a battering from the merciless sun. At the 60 kilometer point, I told Philippe I would never make it if I did not take a short nap in the cool wooded park outside of Forges-les-Eaux. With my indispensable backpack serving as pillow, I dozed off around 20 minutes in this makeshift campground, waking up refreshed and ready to go. "Your rest stops are great for you," Philippe declared with a fraternal smile. "But for me they're hell because I end up taking a smoke."

Philippe, a decade younger than me, led the way on his battered but quicker racing bike, while on climbs I was the pace setter on my reserve mountain bike. From Forges-les-Eaux to Dieppe, it was all voie verte. These "green avenues" in France are mostly former railroad beds, converted into car-free paths, either for bicycles only or to be shared with pedestrians and roller bladers. It was smooth rolling, effortless if it hadn't been for the depleting heat.

The Beer of a Lifetime and its Consequences

Protected by French architectural heritage laws, the abandoned but freshly-painted small-town railroad stations served as colorful landmarks. The only enemy seemed to be the above 90F temperature. It got to a point, at Neufchtel-en-Bray, former industrial town known for pungent cheeses, that we'd earned the right to a cold beer. We got off the Avenue Verte and stopped at the first café, surrounded by abandoned industries. We grabbed the only outdoor table that happened to be in the shade.

We dumped our backpacks under the table and sipped the Stella Artois of a lifetime. No beer commercial could have captured the intense pleasure of my first cold chug. We were off with renewed energy. From Neufchtel to Dieppe was all Voie Verte and I was cruising. Nothing, it seemed, could slow me down. Except! About five kilometers beyond Neufchtel, I remarked to Philippe that I felt as if my biological age had retrogressed to teenager. Why was I so strong?

He looked over at me: "No wonder," he said. "You don't have your backpack!"

After a split-second panic episode, I cooled it. But for a few prescription meds, markers of the aging process, most of my backpack content was replaceable. "Hey Philippe, you don't have to ride back to the café. Wait right here. It's a pretty hangout." "Nonsense," he said. "Of course I'll ride back with you. Saves me from a smoke!" That was the cigarette excuse, but I knew that the extra 10-kilometer round trip for Philippe was a show of solidarity, and would bring our day's total to 130 km, that is, if we made it before dark.

We located my backpack, under the same table, now occupied by two local old-timers, factory workers, cheese mongers, I couldn't say. No time to ask. We were now riding against the clock. Fatigue had become the major enemy, but my strength was renewed when we passed the backstretch of the pretty Dieppe race course, which I duly noted as a future visit. We made it to Dieppe just in time for the sunset.

The following morning, Philippe took me to see fishing villages along the coast. The towering Normandy palisades made for some strenuous climbs from one town to the next. I noticed I was handling the climbs well, while Philippe was paying the consequences from his smoking. Unlike the previous day, we had no clock to beat so the bliss was prolonged. It was the right moment to confirm the words of John F. Kennedy: "Nothing compares to the simple pleasure of riding a bike."

As both bike and train lover, the ride back to Paris on the SNCF Intercities was a pleasure in itself so the Canard Enchaîné weekly on my lap remained unread. I let the psychedelic green rolling hills of Normandy exert their hypnotic effect. A month later, Philippe and I did another overnight, this time to his former country home near Beaugency, on the Loire. It became a pattern match with our Dieppe escapade. The weeks leading up to the trip were beautiful mid-70s weather, and then a rare heat wave arrived exactly at the time of our departure.

Etampes to Beaugency was also a 100+ kilometer trip, with an extra 10-kilometers involving a brief tour of medieval Orleans, a detour around construction between Orleans and the Gothic church at Clery-Saint-André and an extra 5 kilometers between Beaugency, where we dined with Menetou-Salon wine and our 30-Euro truckers' motel, the same place I'd stayed in with Martha.

Heat-distance index

I worked on a mathematical formula for the heat-distance index. In 92F heat, 110 km felt like 165 km! I'll patent the formula. The incremental escalation of my bicycle touring was working out. However, I was missing the strenuous hills that could prepare me for cycling in La Paz, Bolivia.

The air-traffic control researchers had told me that most air accidents are caused by human error. Human error once again was now to cause a bicycle "incident," potentially more perilous than the forgotten backpack or the straight big-truck road I'd chosen to Provins with Martha.

Where's the moon when you need it?

With summer nights holding on to the last rays of sun at 10pm, neither of us had thought it necessary to have functional lights on our bikes. Accustomed to the City of Lights, it did not occur to us that wining and dining in Beaugency past sunset would have consequences. The mere 5-kilometer ride from the restaurant to our motel would take place under a moonless black sky. Once across the bridge from Beaugency, the row of street lights came to an end and the road was suddenly pitch black.

As we inched forward tentatively, we would see the headlights of a car in the distance, but it was not enough light to find a shoulder off the road without plummeting into an embankment. A rare car zooming up from behind us would temporarily light up the road, but what good did that do us since we had to stop and get off to the invisible roadside in order to avoid being barreled over. About halfway back to our motel, I assured Philippe that these 5 kilometers at night were a far greater challenge than the 110 km from Etampes to Beaugency.

Stretching psychological time

Here's how you can extend your life by stretching psychological time. Take this road in the dark! Each minute will seem like the proverbial eternity. Years later, thinking back to this trip, the short ride from Beaugency to our motel feels much longer than the whole route from Paris to Beaugency.

I could see no lights in the distance, as if our motel were in another galaxy hidden by the curvature of space. From its sound, the vehicle now approaching us was a truck. Philippe and I tested the invisible ground at the side of the road to make sure it was relatively flat. It wasn't. This was the first time since I'd known him that the perpetually upbeat Philippe seemed frightened. We experienced a fraternal solidarity that only comes with sharing the same panic. We walked our bikes slowly down an embankment, and perched there until the truck blew past, then inched our way back up to the road.

We pedaled on, more slowly than the snails along the roadside. Finally in the distance we could see the lights of the nearest galaxy, our motel, and edging forward ever so slowly, a flat shoulder of the road finally materialized. As I fell asleep that night, I began counting all the possible unanticipated human errors that could endanger a bike tour:

- departing from a café without picking up my backpack from under the table
- merrily sipping Menetou Salon without considering that it would be too dark to cycle back to the motel after sundown.

The next potential calamity would be as inevitable as it would be unpredictable, and as the air-traffic controllers had explained to me, human error would be to blame.

THE REWARDS OF CLIMBING ...finish going down

My best strategy for doing hills is to begin going up and finish going down. Following bike trips with Martha and Philippe, I had become comfortable with overnight tours. But my eventual goal of cycling in Bolivia had not advanced a whole lot because I'd avoided mountainous regions. I resolved to find a way to practice climbing in geographic contexts where the joy would outweigh the pain.

Many bicycle pleasure seekers decide against doing some of the most satisfying bike tours because they fear the climbs. But my philosopher friend reminds us that, "Hedonism requires an iron discipline and mastery of your desires; following your desires blindly often doesn't lead to pleasurable results." Discipline on the way up, pleasure on the way down.

Discipline on the way up, pleasure on the way down

I was okay with the first line of my personal slogan: As I get older the trips get longer, but not quite sure about a required second line: As I get older the climbs get steeper. But how much of my distaste for uphill cycling in Paris was due to the urban context: car fumes, traffic lights, having to swerve into traffic in order to pass a double-parked delivery truck?

In the 1990s north of La Paz, Bolivia, I'd done hiking to peaks at 16,400 feet (5,000 meters) above sea level, and I was surprisingly quick in getting up, with an acceptable minimum of gasping for air. But a decade later, the age factor had kicked in. In Paris I'd see other cyclists rolling right past me when I was chugging up a hill. I harbored a Thoreau-derived expectation that rural climbs would somehow be easier than the urban ones. I had a chance to test it out when my wife and I were visiting friends in a remote village of less than 300 inhabitants, called Parnans, in the Drôme region of France, the foothills to the Alps.

Nearly 200 meters in altitude above Parnans was a pretty cliff-side village called Montmiral, reachable over the winding route D323. My thoughts at the time: If I look up and can see a beautiful place, I can get there, as if my eyes were a secret source of energy. Our intention during the four day stay was afternoon mountain hiking with Julie and Bob, packing a picnic lunch. That left my mornings free to go out on Bob's sporty red bicycle.

On my first morning out I took one look at D323 winding up into the woods and wimped out, "deciding" in the name of geographical correctness, to first get to know the flatter surrounding context.

On the second morning, after touring and detouring, I finally set out to climb the 6.5 kilometers to Montmiral. I made it two thirds of the way up, stopped to admire an idyllic panorama, looked up at the hairpin turns, and chose to return to Parnans, promising to come back the following morning. I needed to do the whole climb without stopping.

Last swing after two strikes!

On the third morning, with the long-term dream of Bolivia Cordillera climbing at stake, there was no turning back. I was learning that even a steep climb, 178 meters in 6.5 kilometers, was made easier by hairpin turns, where each bend in the road acted as a landing on a staircase. The climb actually began 5km before Montmiral, with the average gradient from that point on of nearly 4%.

The simple answer was to keep pedaling, and that I did. I made it to the top, found a café with a terrace lookout, and rejoiced with the timeless green-valley view. From an old photo of the same panoramic view, I could see that little had changed in the valley since 1947.

Like the Hedonist told me, discipline leading to pleasure. The invigorating, gravity-assisted downhill return incorporated a message: each climb will have its reward.

CHASING ALAN FOR A THOUSAND KILOMETERS

As the calendar months flipped by, my goals evolved, acquiring loftier aspirations. At age 20, each year was 1/20th of my life. Approaching 70, each had shrunk to 1/70th of the same life. As time slipped away, the number of meds in my backpack increased, from one to ten. Also increasing were my rest stops between segments of a journey. Martha and I would engage in dueling competitions to see which one of us carried more medications during an outing.

My answer to this uncompromising reality was to reaffirm my long-term objectives.

- To cycle regularly in and around La Paz, Bolivia, at 12,000 feet above sea level.

- "Get out on the open road and don't look back."

In the realms of both hiking and cycling, I was thinking both LONGER and HIGHER, and hoping that the longer would eventually make the higher easier. I pedaled forward, using Monk's Brilliant Corners as a rolling mantra during a few solo bike tours. Alan Kennedy, art collector and curator, was also a Monk fan.

He'd read some of my horse racing books, discovering that he and I both bet on the ponies, loved bike riding and were avid readers of Charles Bukowski. We shared our common interests over a drink at Café de Beaux Arts in the 5th Arrondissement, where we decided to bicycle to as many race tracks as possible, blending two of our avocations into a single package.

Two people can have everything in common and still become a mismatch as a bicycle team. Alan was six years younger and a few inches taller, his long legs transforming him into a gazelle on a bike. With Alan my climbing began to improve. It was also with Alan that I discovered how slow I was. Not used to looking back, Alan would go on his merry way and then discover he'd left me behind. Sooner or later he'd stop and wait up for me.

When I caught up, I'd suggest that we might not work out as a team since I was slowing him down. Alan, influenced by reflective Asian art, respected the idea of taking one's time, though his legs did not always agree. "Our goal is to get there and enjoy the trip," he'd say. "As long as we arrive, it makes no difference how fast. We're fine."

One of our earlier defiant climbs was in the Picardie region, from Pont Ste Maxence at the Oise River, up through the forest on the way to medieval Senlis. This small segment of a 300 kilometer bike tour became a peak experience. Forest custodian Michel Urly told me that the gradient in some parts of the forest routes was as much as 10%. Unlike my climb to Montmiral, the Senlis forest climb was straight, with no hairpin reprieves.

Alan lost me on the way up, but eventually I perceived his elongated silhouette at the top of the hill. As if I were riding Sancho Panza's donkey, I made it to the top without stopping, but with a wounded ego. No problem keeping up with him on the breezy downhill glide into Senlis.

Riding short-term, thinking long

Fueled by this and other climbs with Alan, I set my long-term sights on the canyon roads around La Paz. Back in Paris, I would spread out a map of La Paz from the Bolivian Instituto Geográfico Militar. I identified a particular urban climb in La Zona Sur with a minimum of motor traffic and a maximum of rough canyon landscapes, and etched it in my mind as first test against Andean gravity, 200 meters to be climbed in only 4 kilometers! For La Paz, that would be my beginner's climb. (You measure the average gradient by the distance traveled vertically (200 m) divided by the distance traveled horizontally (4km = 4000 m): 4000 / 200 = .05 or 5%.)

The Senlis climb was an indicator that I could handle a single climb in La Paz, that is, if La Paz were at sea level. The unknown variable would be the altitude. For racing purposes, climbing parcours are graded according to the average slope or gradient, from Category 4, the easiest, to Category 1, the most difficult, with an hors catégorie being even tougher than Category 1. For a 4 km distance, Category 4 would be less than a 4% slope. Category 3 would be 2-4km @ 6% or 4-6km @ 4%, exactly my intended beginner ride. Category 2 would be 5-10 km @ 5-7% slope. Forget Category 1.

The Pont Sainte-Maxence-Senlis climb qualified as a Category 3. I played around with the probabilities. The projected La Paz beginner's climb, if I extended it up another 100 meters to the rural town of Huayllani, would fit within Category 2, once the 12,000 feet above sea level was factored in. (A higher altitude raises the category.) No Tour de France climb, either in the Alps or the Pyrénées, comes near the 3600 meter altitude of La Paz.

Reading the map again and again was going to make the climbs easier once I was out on the real road. Let the energy enter through the eyes and then gather force as it spirals into the legs and lungs. I convinced myself that if I could make it through 1,000 km laterally in pursuit of a gazelle like Alan, then I should be able to do 300 meters vertically in La Paz.

In 2010 Alan and I accepted the challenge of a 1,000 kilometer charity ride, coinciding neatly with the 21 days of the Tour de France. Sue Finley, mastermind of the project and publisher of *ThoroughbredDailyNews*, gave us a daily blog and website to receive donations for the Thoroughbred Retirement Foundation, which finds homes for horses that might face slaughter at the end of their careers, and which also uses the healing of broken-down horses as therapy for people on the edge of personal disaster, notably inmates at prison farms.

One detractor asked pointedly how we were working on a charity for horses when so many human beings were in need. Never mind that I'd spent a lifetime on human rights issues. I went right to the grain: "Using animals for entertainment and then sending them off to slaughter is an attack on our own humanity. Besides, we too are animals!" Before accepting the challenge, I mentioned to Alan that, as his perpetual pursuer, my self-esteem was vulnerable. Once again he assured me our goal was simply to arrive.

Deflated tire, deflated ego

One early segment of our long haul found us revisiting the Compiegne race course. On the way to that splendid track in the middle of a forest and near the serene Oise River, I found myself cycling ahead of Alan… all the way! Was he purposely slowing in order to boost my confidence? I began entertaining a splendid illusion, that all this cycling had reduced my real age compared to my chronological age … until I discovered the truth. Alan's back tire was half flat. In all we were to visit 13 different race tracks. Our goal was to raise $20,000. We would pay our own expenses, lodging and food along the way, hopefully from profits in our race betting. Of course, by getting to these tracks by bike, we'd have zero fuel expenses. My blogs served as a medium to advance the larger ecological cause in a mellow, non-sectarian way: that human energy was underestimated as a sustainable answer to the climate crisis.

If we cycled the projected 100 hours on this trip, that would add 4 days to our lives.

The challenge was to cycle for the same 21 days of the Tour de France, in order to gain the maximum media exposure for fundraising. We were even written up in sports blogs at ESPN and the New York Times, quite a feat for a non-athlete like me. The thousand kilometers we were to cover would only be a quarter of the real Tour mileage, but we'd be spending more hours on the road than the supermen tour riders, thanks to our human pace, for which the only doping was a cup of coffee.

I recalled the research statistic that "every hour of cycling adds one hour to your life." If we cycled the projected 100 hours on this trip, that would add 4 days to our lives. There is always something in it for the person who engages in a charity, even in cases that seem to be pure altruism. We had to do 1,000 kilometers for the charity but we'd have fun doing it. To maximize the fundraising fanfare, we were to arrive behind the winners' podium of the Tour de France at the Arc de Triomphe, at the same time as the Tour riders hung out there.

By staying in family-run hotels or B&Bs in non-tourist areas, lodging costs were minimal. We preferred the travel-light mode of bike touring as opposed to totally self-sufficient touring with panniers and camping gear. But this put us at risk each night of not finding a place to stay. We'd be visiting race tracks during the day and would have to do much of our cycling in late afternoon and early evening, up to the 10pm twilight time.

On two occasions we found ourselves in the twilight zone in the middle of nowhere, with no nearby lodging. The first time, as I prepared to sleep outdoors in a windy nook in front of the village church, Alan got on his cell phone and found a rural B&B within two kilometers. Bike lights don't help if there are no street lights. We squinted through the corn fields to take advantage of the final hint of what they call "astronomical twilight," taking care to not go off an embankment on an unseen curve in the road.

Our second twilight zone episode hit us in the Mayenne region. We'd intended to get to Angers for the night. But that was 92 kilometers from the race course at Chateaubriant. We left the track "early" at 3pm, but still had to stop at an internet café to write the blog for the charity ride. The heat got worse as the afternoon progressed and our forced rest stops increased in frequency. I'd mapped the trip to pass through a cool forest but once out in the open, it became apparent that we would not make it to Angers.

The terrain broke into hills. Though the gradients were not extreme, the climbs were straight and extended, with no respite. At about 9pm we arrived at a town and asked for a hotel. None. At 9:40 we struggled into another town. No hotel. We were told there might be a small village gite type lodging in the next town but it was nearly too late to cycle. We had seven kilometers to cycle at maximum possible speed, in order to get from La Poueze to Saint-Clément-de-la-Place before the astronomical twilight had vanished.

Bat's Motel

My adrenalin took over, while the terrain helped us by flattening out. The temperature was finally dropping and the pastoral farmscapes were sparkling in the dimming rays of sun. Monet would have stopped to paint.

Even if we found the gite, we had no idea if there'd be an available room. This time I was able to keep up with Alan, pedal for pedal, even taking off in front of him for a spell, humming "Twilight Time" around the bend, sounding like The Platters, drowning out the crickets. Entering the town we came across a woman watering her front-yard flower bed. Was there a hotel? Yes, a gîte, she said, pointing us in the right direction.

Bats swooped across the road, diving for mosquitoes between the village church and the cornfields. No one answered our knocks on the hardwood door at the small gite, while the agitated bats above obeyed no traffic rules. Half a block away, we found the lights of a bar, people singing. One of the crooners was the owner of the gite. He gave us a key, told us to pay later, then went back to his chorus. If they'd sung *Twilight Time*, I'd have joined in.

The place looked like a rural tool shed: but atop the narrow stairway with no handrail, a door opened into large room, with grainy woodwork and two comfortable beds. We'd found our Bat's Motel. From then on, all the good things about cycling came true, including a visit to the Villandry castle gardens near Tours. At the last race course of our visit, Vichy, the track management had us take our bikes up onto the podium in the winners' circle, with the track announcer giving a spirited discourse in favor of our noble cause.

I'd been able to pay for hotels and food along the way with my moderate profits from the horse race betting. We didn't reach our charity goal but did get past $12,000. Not bad!

Too early to celebrate

Some 10 miles from our finish line at the Arc de Triomphe, I felt a slow leak in my back tire. Alan had gone ahead to secure a spot behind the Arc, taking the tire repair kit with him. I limped on, finally deciding to walk the bike for the final 4 kilometers. Once arrived, there was still enough air in the tire to do some wobbly victory loops, with Alan and I getting filmed by his daughter. Thousands of people were hanging around after the official Tour ceremonies but none of them were aware that Alan and I were the real winners of our own tour de France.

In a stretch of the imagination, I reasoned that if I could make it past 1,000 km laterally, then I should be able to do 300 meters vertically in La Paz. I came out of it with my long-term goals intact, proving as well that doing charity work can be self-serving, and that's quite okay.

On our final scoreboard we learned:

Minus 1,000 kilometers of motorized tourism +1,000 km by bike = 200 kilogram reduction in carbon emissions

THE SPOKES METHOD:
WHAT IS OUR HOME BUT AN EXTENDED CAMPGROUND!

"We ride to make familiar places new again." (People for Bikes)

Most folks who yearn to get out and tour on two wheels lament about the responsibility factor, as Robert Frost reminded us: the woods are lovely, dark and deep /but I have promises to keep ...

During periods laden with promises to keep, when longer tours are out of the question, the answer is to use one's residence as a home base, doing day tours in every possible direction, like the spokes of a wheel. You'd be surprised what you can discover within 50 kilometers of home.

I've found a way to keep up appearances as a respected member of society, by escaping in the morning and then rejoining the world in the afternoon. In my region I can leave before 9am, discover a new village or a funky suburb, and be back in time for my afternoon responsibilities.

"But with the spokes method," one naysayer told me, "I'll miss the camping part of bike touring."

Sorry to say this but the place where you live is merely an extended campground. It has no more permanence than a tent pitched in the woods above a beautiful canyon; it just lasts a dash longer, less than a blink in geological or cosmic time. Nothing against the joys of camping, but the Spokes method is a backup for those periods when we have no choice but to stay in contact with the world. I can see good reasons for camping beyond the reach of cell phone contact during Olympic games, election campaigns and graduation ceremonies. I plan to be out camping instead of attending my own funeral.

We first discovered the spokes method from our previous residence on the east side of Paris. I did not want to repeat the experience of George Orwall in his Down and Out in Paris, so I had to remain on call in the gig economy. On free days, Martha and I merely needed to cross the beautiful Vincennes forest and we could descend upon the riverfront bike "highway" known as Bords de la Marne, which took us all the way to the pretty village of Lagny and the countryside beyond, 27.5 kilometers in two hours. From our same apartment, we also had access to another waterfront bike path along the Canal de l'Ourcq, which took us through the refreshing Sévran Forest to Ville Parisis and the countryside beyond, 22.5 kilometers in an hour and 30 minutes.

Each of these waterway exit corridors offered side trips along the way, multiplying the number of destinations, while each allowed us the option of cycling for the return or putting our bike on a train. Suburban sprawl was thus alleviated and the French countryside was within remarkably convenient reach.

From my current "campsite" in Clichy just north of the Périphérique ring road, using the spokes method, summer of 2017, I rode 1,600 kilometers (1,000 miles) visiting classic French beaux villages, climbing into deep forests such as Montmorency, stopping at historic castles, and visiting art towns like Van Gogh's final resting place in Auvers-Sur-Oise, exactly 25 km from my front door, only a 50 km round trip.

During those thousand miles, I rode 28 different spokes or branches of spokes, all beginning at our apartment. That's a longer distance than from New York to Madison, Wisconsin, longer than from Los Angeles to El Paso, Texas. It's farther than the route of the train they call The City of New Orleans, 925 miles, Chicago to New Orleans.

And speaking of trains, I cheated on a couple of occasions, taking the bicycle into a train for the return back to base camp. Such blended transport, bike plus train, allowed me to cycle a longer distance on the spoke. I came across dozens of sweet or grungy places I'd never seen.

Robert Frost wrote that, Two roads diverged in a wood / and I took the one less traveled by. Good choice, old man, but with the spokes method, you can go back and take the other one as well. This is the "sauntering" method used on foot from his base in Concord, Massachusetts by Thoreau in his "Walking" (1862).

Further advantages from spokes touring: you discover fewer places than you would on a cross-continental tour but you get to know those places more intimately. By repeating the same trip several times, I made new discoveries, like:

- the cormorants, terns and herons at a secluded marshland squeezed within an industrial zone

- the old man in his 90s who takes long walks with a cane to the park, where he becomes a storyteller for children on school field trips

- car-free routes passing through the immense forest of Montmorency, where I can picnic at my personal "Walden" ponds or gather chestnuts in October

You get the idea. In fact, my 28 spokes can be multiplied by ten, for on each known route I make sure I break the routine, detour, and diverge (following advice for staving off Alzheimer's. I'll never repeat a spoke route without trying something different: a new café along the way, a river towpath, a little village in steadfast resistance of suburban highrise blight.

You will ask, "What if there are no beautiful or adventurous places within a 50-kilometer radius of my home?" Don't be so sure. One of my spokes tours takes me to an area referred to by Fox News as a no-go zone, yet I discovered some stunning examples of industrial architecture as well as a bird sanctuary.

If you live in the Los Angeles area of Southern California, for example, you can use a bike-friendly Metrolink commuter train network to deposit yourself near state parks, and still get back the same day. Train tickets are expensive but seniors get an automatic half-price discount.

Alright, let's stipulate that some of you live in a place that simply does not lend itself to bicycle touring. Then we try alternative spokes tours. Take off between four days and a week and stay in a place where cycling is a great pleasure and rental bikes are available. I've done an extended spokes bike tour with Martha, with medieval Bruges, in Belgium as the base camp. Bikes are the priority form of transport in Bruges for citizens of all ages.

Most cycling outside of Bruges is an easy spin along canal tow paths lined with shade trees, passing attractive hamlets, castles, ancient fortified farm houses, picturesque bridges, centuries-old churches, and the polder farmlands between Bruges and the sea. The cost of renting a bike for a whole day is moderate. This spokes tour included a ride to the beach for a day, only 30 kilometers round trip. We got a feel for what it's like to exist below sea level when we had to climb slightly uphill from the polder to the beach.

The first-class alternative spokes-tour

Consider a more preposterous alternative. Let's say you've got a week to vacation in a European city, including touring in the countryside with a rental car. According to travel expert Rick Steves, the average weekly cost for a low-cost rental car is $580, including gas and insurance.

For half that price you can buy (yes, I said, buy!) a basic but solid bicycle from a local shop. You're saving money and at the same time getting healthy exercise you would not get from behind a steering wheel of a rental car. Comparable trips could be taken in and around bike-friendly cities such as Portland (Oregon), Seattle (Washington) or Minneapolis-Saint Paul (Minnesota), to name a few.

When it's time to leave, thanks to the savings from not renting a car, you can afford to donate the bike to the local cycling advocacy group that needs it for its bicycle education classes. This would qualify as low-impact tourism: sustainable travel that directly benefits local communities and is respectful of the environment.

IF KEROUAC HAD TRAVELED BY BICYCLE

In *On the Road*, if Jack Kerouac had traveled by bicycle, Cormac McCarthy might never have written his great novel, *The Road*, fifty years later in 2006. Only one word separates the two titles but it's nothing to do with literary influence. The connection is hidden. "There was nowhere to go but everywhere, so just keep on rolling," Kerouac wrote, suggesting that planning was a bad idea. Marcelo Dasque, 21st century bicycle traveler exemplifies the Kerouac message.

Morning haze, El Alto, Bolivia, 13,000 feet above sea level: I ask Marcelo, "where are you headed?" He shoots back a question: "What do you recommend, Lake Titicaca or the Peruvian border?" Like Kerouac, Marcelo shuns planning. He'd slept the night before as a guest in the fire station. He's been on the road for 9 months.

In the novel *On The Road*, Sal Paradise (Kerouac) and his friend Dean Moriarty hit the road in search of unbridled freedom, hitchhiking, taking a bus or driving a car, and looking for the best in people. Like a Kerouac character, Marcelo is proud to depend on the good will of people along the way.

The road novel, most critics agree, is an American genre. In fact, the first road novels came from Spain: *Lazarillo de Tormes* (1554), author unknown, and of course, *Don Quixote de la Mancha* (1605 and 1615), by Cervantes. The *Quixote* and *On the Road* share an obstinate romanticism. Along with rock'n'roll, Kerouac's novel rattled the Calvinism of the fifties. (A few years after reading it, I was moved to carve out my own on-the-road, hitchhiking from México City to Cuzco, Perú and back.) Between 1960 and 1964 this episodic novel catalyzed another work of literature, the 116 TV episodes of *Route 66*.

In *Route 66*, an indispensable Chevy Corvette is a medium for two travel partners to experience adventures from town to town. The Corvette becomes the third character. In the first episode, the Corvette owner exclaims: "It's more than just a car to me!" Surprise! The program's sponsor was Chevrolet.

Miracle: with each new season, the two young travelers find themselves in a new Corvette model. We never learn how this happens. Imagine Don Quixote each year riding a new Rocinante. Under the influence of *On The Road*, *Route 66* contributes to the cult of the automobile. We learn subliminally that we are nothing without a car. No woman would pay attention to me if I arrive by bus, subway, or bicycle.

On the big screen, heroes drive potent cars. James Bond drives. Steve McQueen drives. And later, Nicolas Cage drives. One notable exception was Richard Kimble, in *The Fugitive,* who hitchhiked or traveled by bus. But fugitive Kimble had no choice.

Years later we saw Forrest Gump, jogging across the country. But Gump was presented as an abnormal. Normal people continued to drive across the screen. During this period suburban sprawl was booming. Housing developments were intentionally implanted far from viable public transportation. These "communities" were void of street life, distant from useful shopping, and zoned against night life. The only exit from the blandness was the compulsory automobile. *Route 66* offered an immediate escape for suburbanites from their cloistered living rooms. Meanwhile, urban centers were reconstituted to give total priority to the car. Los Angeles would dedicate 14% of its surface to parking lots. Even Andy Warhol could not squeeze art from a parking lot.

In the mid 60s, a second wave of counterculture, less individualistic than the Beats of Kerouac, embraced anti-war and ecological issues, but the critical spirit of the time failed to offer an alternative to automobile totalitarianism. The Doors' icon, Jim Morrison, loved his Blue Lady, a Shelby Mustang. Car songs proliferated with the Beach Boys and diversified with low riders, *Mustang Sally* (Wilson Pickett) and *Let Me Ride* (Dr Dre).

Pollution blanketed Mexico City, Lima, and Sao Paulo, while with increasing CO_2 emissions, Andean glaciers trickled to death. Millions of refugees escaped the ravages of extreme climate. The frightening dystopian scenario for Cormac McCarthy's *The Road* in 2006 became increasingly plausible.

In 2016, investigative reporter Jad Lindgaard wrote in Mediapart (France) that approximately 2,500 people die each year in Paris, my city of residence, because of the air they breathe. And we are not Mexico City. McCarthy has never told us if the dystopia in The Road resulted from war or ecological catastrophe. But for Andrew O'Hagan The Road is" the first great masterpiece of the globally warmed generation" while George Monbiot calls it "the most important environmental book ever written."

In *The Road*, a father and son travel on foot, north to south, in search of a ray of sun, coughing their way through landscapes of abandoned cars and acid rain, while dehumanized marauders violently capture the few resources that have not disappeared. In the extreme, human flesh becomes one of those resources. Finally a novel (and superb film) where the characters travel on foot! Do we require a great catastrophe in order to use human energy for our travels?

We had to wait 25 years for the cycling version of Kerouac's *On the Road: Latinoamérica. Crónica de un Viaje en Bicicleta*, yet to be translated to English, by the Basque writer Jesús López de Dicastillo. This pioneer of bicycle voyaging pedaled from Mexico City to Brasilia. After writing about it, he continued his expeditions, by bike but also on foot. López de Dicastillo began his far-reaching, emission-free travels after having suffered an identity crisis provoked by his work as an automobile engineer. His book did not trigger a cycling version of *Route 66.* But it inspired an adventurous spirit in fellow Basque, Lorenzo Rojo: The book "showed me that doing such a thing was mad, was exciting and, above all, was possible."

"Just a few years later, in 1987, I cycled for 6 months in Latin America. In 1997 I started a new trip that is still going on" (The Next Challenge, 23 May 2014). A former teacher of language and literature, Rojo says: "I travel with an old bicycle, an austere budget and still the same desire to see the world, and maybe even more than when I began." (*MunduaBarrena Blog*) Nowadays the new Kerouacs, following the paths of Lorenzo Rojo and Jesús López de Dicastillo, pedal across countries and continents. They are young and old, men and women (the Beats were men only). Dr. Kate Leeming, author of *Njinga: Breaking the Cycle of Africa*, cycled 22,000 kilometers across Africa and that was only the starter for her legendary cross-continent rides.

The car has been a symbol of competition. The only competition of the bicycle voyager is with oneself, as Bolivian bicycle advocate Gina Muñoz Villegas explains, referring to a 70-kilometer event: "the Samaipata climb." "I don't participate with a desire to compete. I do it as a challenge to myself, with the purpose of completing the climb in the most spiritual way possible. For me, riding uphill to Samaipata is a type of meditation, a celebration of life itself. Cycling uphill between the green mountains is like merging with them, a prolonged breath that liberates me from the routine of daily life."

Chilean bicycle traveler Aldo Orpianesi adds: "One aspect that separates us from professional cycling is the lack of competition. We are not concerned about competing." (*Mas Deportes*, 27 Marzo, 2016)

The association Randonneurs USA explains: "When riders participate in randonneuring events, they are part of a long tradition that goes back to the beginning of the sport of cycling in France and Italy. Friendly camaraderie, not competition, is the hallmark of randonneuring." (*rusa.org*)

Like Kerouac, bicycle travelers get around with limited funds. They use web pages like *warmshowers.org* that provide free lodging with families that enjoy welcoming cyclists. Each bicycle traveler has a philosophy. For me it's simple: the open road is more liberating when it's done with human energy. We have reached a period of parallel realities. From one vision we see, in Cormac McCarthy's *The Road*, a dystopian voyage where savage competition allows for the survival of only a few.

From a parallel configuration, bicycle travelers, and backpackers as well, prove it's possible to cross continents without polluting, with joyful frugality and with generous help from people along the route.

(Some material in this chapter previously appeared in Suburbano.net.)

III

BIKE AND WALK

Inutile de vous expliquer

BICYCLE THIEVES, TIME THEFT

Professional thieves have managed to separate my bike from its dependable lock on three occasions, with state-of-the-art cutting tools and with In-and-Out-Burger efficiency. On the police reports, I declared that my bicycle was stolen.

What was really stolen was my time, the time I used to efficiently and pleasurably get to and from work. Given my more than 6,000 hours of bike commuting in nearly two decades and the 4,000 times I'd parked the bike during that period, three thefts meant that my bike was stolen less than .003 percent of the time. Furthermore, the bicycle was replaceable. But what about the loss of my time?

After each robbery I needed a good week to shop for a new bike. During the transition period I vowed to recover much of the time that had been stolen from me, by walking to and from my jobs instead of taking the train. This may sound illogical since using the metro is quicker than walking. But the underground is a type of non-space with its somber stretches of dead time. On my feet above ground, I regain control of my sense of time and place. Along with a worthless sawed-off lock, the thieves left me something of value: an implicit message that I should vary my physical activity.

Walking is a weight-bearing exercise that complements the fitness we derive from non-weight-bearing cycling. Balancing commuter time between walking and cycling becomes a low-key biathlon. Between my apartment and my teaching job at Sciences-Po it was 37 minutes by bike but an hour and 20 minutes on foot. I lost some linear time on foot but gained it back with intangibles. Whizzing by bike across the Seine over the stony Pont Neuf (built in 1604) blurs certain sensorial delights that come into focus at the slower pace of walking. Cycling and walking are mutually supportive, for fitness, aesthetics and the environment.

Prior to the theft, I viewed cycling as independent of walking. In the frequent climbs I did with Alan Kennedy, for example, only once did I have to get off my bike and push it up the remaining twenty meters of a hill. I got off that bike as if I were breaking the most important of the 10 commandments: Thou shalt not push thy bike up a hill.

Now in La Paz, Bolivia, I gazed up into the ascending urban-canyon route that I'd highlighted in red on my map. I could now actually see the Tour de France level gradients and feel the oxygen-deprived altitude. Intimidated, I envisioned the potential obliteration of my self-esteem. It seemed inevitable that, at some point, I would have to get off that bike and walk. I resolved to do everything possible to outwit the gradients, by activating the extra gears in my mind.

LA PAZ: SECOND CHANCE

In my high school days in New York, where all the kids in the neighborhood were gamblers, I learned to evaluate my living probabilities in terms of poker. For my new endeavor I now perceived a hand with two aces, two kings and a lowly three. The good hand came from a radical change in the deep canyon city La Paz and the high-plain satellite city above it, known as El Alto, 13,000 feet above sea level.

My two aces reflected a new strategic advantage: bicycles were now admitted in the cabins of the aerial cable cars of Mi Teleférico, a bold transportation system spearheaded by the national government and backed by the president, which dramatically reduced both commuting distances and carbon emissions. The two kings referred to a complementary strategic advantage: new bike racks on the public bus system called Pumakatari, established by the mayor of La Paz in order to provide an alternative to the anarchistic, uberistic mini-bus system, in which individual driver-entrepreneurs fought it out for limited space on the streets, to the detriment of public transit. The new Pumakatari system was the public empire striking back.

The three referred to the number of kilometers I'd still have to climb from the nearest Teleférico station to our apartment. That three could be exchanged for another ace or king if only I became adept at cycling up steep hills, against the push-back of a silent enemy: the altitude.

The two literally ground-breaking transit systems needed co-ordination between a president and a mayor who belonged to opposing political parties and for the most part they'd set their differences aside to make it happen. These bike-friendly services were initiated thanks in part to the advocacy of pro-cycling groups such as Masa Crítica La Paz (similar to my bike association in Paris) and an NGO called Swiss Contact.

Suddenly, I could partake of blended transportation, bike-in-public-transport for uphills and bike alone for downhills. With the Teleférico in particular, time and space were unraveled into a new dimension. Back in France the revolutionary high speed train (train à grande vitesse) broke a speed barrier by mastering Newtonian physics in order to go faster. In a more quantum dimension, the Teleférico cabins are breaking a time-and-space barrier as they glide over the contorted canyon city. They get to their destination sooner by going slower!

In the initial euphoria of both Teleférico and Pumakatari, I'd neglected the obvious facts. Uphill: I'd still have to do climbing to various areas unreached by public transport. Downhill was not nearly as easy as one would imagine, and in fact, in parts of the city it could be treacherous. On a descent I'd have to deal with daredevil gradients and then multi-task by providing instant, on-the-road "education" to aggressive truck and minibus drivers about the rights of a bike rider.

On my second day in La Paz, I went for advice to the workshop of Aniceto, who was referred to me by a British cyclist acquaintance as one of the best bike mechanics he'd ever known. Aniceto had once worked as a mechanic for the U.S. military.

Approaching 80 years of age, Aniceto still did mountain biking in the rough Andean foothills around the city. He suggested that before I made an expensive purchase, I should start out with a low-cost bicycle. He pointed out which of the cheaper bike brands offered the best quality. Only after I knew that I could manage cycling in La Paz should I graduate to a better bike, he explained, which could be selected based on particular needs that I would only be able to define after experiencing the terrain on two wheels.

Prior to my first outing, I sat at the kitchen table of our apartment on 23rd Street in Calacoto and rewrote a 5-step plan I'd formulated on the flight from Miami. In descending order of difficulty (10 to 1):

- Incrementally increase my climbing until I could ascend 300 meters within the 6 kilometers it would take me to reach the outpost community of Huayllani: an average 5% gradient with some 10% stretches(10)

- Do the breathtaking and nerve-testing descent from 4,000 meters at El Alto, down the Llojeta road to 3,255 m at Plaza Humboldt. (8)

- Identify, through on-the-road research, the safest commuter route between downtown La Paz, and the Zona Sur, by far the most traveled corridor in the city. (7)

- Join the La Paz Critical Mass cycling advocates on a Sunday morning excursion. (3)

- If I managed the above four steps, then spread the message in the media: if bicycle commuting can be done in the intimidating city of La Paz by an old man in his seventies who has no particular athletic skills, then it will be possible in any city in the world. (2)

In advance I understood that my goal number one, climbing hundreds of meters over steep gradients at an obscene altitude, was beyond my physical capabilities and that I'd be depending on the questionable theory of mind over matter in order to defy Newtonian physics.

I entered the challenge with an unstable mix of elation and trepidation, as well as a far less noble fear that I'd become a less agile version of Mr. Bean on a bike, a caricature of the caricature.

THE FINAL RESTING PLACE

I set out on my morning climbs incrementally, the way the Wright brothers began testing the first airplane. My personal Kitty Hawk was a landscape of mainly middle class and affluent communities implanted within a canyon corridor with jagged perpendicular walls on either side. A number of narrow rivers flowed down from the glaciers in the Cordillera, and I was like a salmon with defective fins, flailing against the flow.

My first huff-and-puff "increments" were embarrassingly short: day 1, to Alexander's café, a single kilometer from our apartment (but farther than the 120 feet of Orville Wright's first flight in 1903); day 2, a visit to Aniceto's bike shop, about a kilometer and a half. I was taking a longer checkerboard route that allowed for climbing one block, turning left on a flat residential street for another, then turning right to climb a third block. This checker-boarding stretch eluded vehicle traffic and eased the average gradient, but beyond Aniceto's workshop, I'd be forced onto the main road.

"You'd better hope to die because I won't take care of you if you survive a stroke"

Martha warned me: "If you get knocked out by the altitude, you'd better hope to die because I'm not taking care of you if you get a stroke." She'd earned the right to invitations on tough-love talk shows.

On climbing day 3 I decided to cycle to a niece's house, bordering a canyon wall, 2 ½ km from our apartment. I made it for 2 km until my breathing began to gallop. No theme song, not even Coltrane's *A Love Supreme*, not even the Bolivian National Anthem could prevent this shortness of breath from overtaking me.

A hologram of my French cardiologist, dressed as a cop, called out ARRÊT, which could have meant either "stop" or "arrest" as in "cardiac arrest." The advice was unnecessary. I had no choice but to cave in, abruptly, at the side of the stone-walled rivulet just across a short pedestrian bridge from a building called Asilo San Ramón. There was an intoxicating delight in sitting down and purging the stress. But what was this bizarre place? And why had I been pulled over by a subconscious cop at this particular bend in the road?

No soft-leather armchair could compare with my stone wall perch. I began reviving myself with instant sophrology. "What is this place?" I asked a woman who had just come out of the building. She said she'd visited her elderly mother. She recommended it (to me?) as "the best home in La Paz for old folks who can no longer take care of themselves."

So this was it! I'd been forced off the road right in front of the institution that threatened to take me in for my final days. This was not a metaphor. It was right there, tangible, the gateway to a Final Resting Place. A middle-aged man took his father out in a wheel chair. The man in the chair looked not a day older than me. If I suffered a stroke from this self-inflicted insanity, who would be pushing my wheel chair? Not Martha!

Gradually the thumping subsided and my breathing returned to near normal. I considered returning home in defeat. Instead I vowed to rebel against, or at least postpone, the final resting place. I got on the bike and continued climbing until I made it to our niece's house. The cycling felt strangely relieving after the forced rest. No one was home. It was a quiet street and I could hear the gurgling river and gaze at the limestone canyon wall vaulting above, an occasional pine tree encroaching in a nook. This could have been the facade of a neo-medieval troglodyte cathedral. Gaudi would be impressed!

My return was, of course, all downhill, with awesomely implausible canyon country spreading out before me, as I harmonized with the swoop of the condor. Back in the 1890s, magazine articles predicted that "the flying machine problem is liable to be solved by bicycle inventors" (Fast Company, 8 July 2016) and many aviation pioneers, including the Wright brothers, were dedicated cyclists.

I verified that my wheels still touched the ground but in my oxygen-deprived heart, as millions of red blood cells were gathering to expand and reproduce, I was flying. I waved a defiant good-bye to the old-age home, soared past Aniceto's shop with no need for repairs, floated by Alexander's café with a promise to land there soon for a well-earned cinnamon roll, and then I was home.

After an hour of chilling out, I took my blood pressure. Normal. Pulse? Only a point or two higher than normal. I showed the screen to Martha, my not-so-subtle way to say, Told ya so! "You may not get a stroke," she said, "but you'll waste away with all the calories you're burning." She quoted various medical journals. "You absolutely need a big lunch."

At high altitudes, simply breathing is a weight-loss exercise

Up the street was a ma-and-pa bistro where we sat next to the waitress's bicycle. Alexandra served us a thick quinoa soup as a starter, and then a copious main dish featuring crispy grilled trout. We served ourselves at an all-you-can-eat salad bar, with Martha picking out the "antioxidants" for me. Anything that might postpone having to push me in a wheelchair. No question that fresh beets are tastier than their canned look-alike impostors. And for dessert, throw in a chocolate mousse.

Martha assured me that there was no such thing as eating too much in La Paz. At this altitude, even the body at rest burns more calories, just by breathing harder! My post-excursion analysis was leading to a great reckoning. Nothing to do with an old-age home. I'd learned that stopping to rest was a way of getting to my destination. I recalled Alan Kennedy's fraternal words of encouragement. "Getting there is what counts."

Accidental interval training

Martha would often implore me to do some prerequisite medical research before taking physical risks. I got it in reverse. I first took the risks and then studied up on what I'd done. That afternoon in an internet café, I learned that what I'd just experimented with was a form of high-intensity interval training (HIIT): "Alternating short periods of intense exercise with recovery periods of passive or mild-intensity movement," according to numerous sources. My checkerboarding strategy, alternating flat side streets with blocks rising in my intended direction, fit loosely within the definition of HIIT, as did my taking a rest (recovery period) and then continuing.

With recovery periods now an option, I was ready for the next increment: the Achumani football stadium, 3550 meters above sea level (12,000 feet), 200 plus meters higher in altitude than our apartment.

IS IT HERESY TO GET OFF A BIKE AND PUSH WHEN IT GETS TOO STEEP?

I made sure not to wake up Martha, enjoyed grainy chamillo toast with butter, a banana, and a glass of cold milk, got my bike out of the basement storage bin, walked it up two flights of stairs and was off at 6:30am while the air still had a refreshing cold bite to it and annoying minibuses were few and far between. Once past my niece's house, the gradient got steeper. The day's target, the Achumani stadium, practice pitch for Bolivia's legendary football (soccer) club founded in 1908, The Strongest, was the positive antidote to the ominous old-age home.

My wife comes from a football family. Her oldest brother, Vicente, was known as the Andean Arrow for his skill at diving to block shots, the first Bolivian to play professionally in Argentina. All of Martha's nephews are Strongest supporters. A symbolic destination provides an extra lift for the bike rider.

I labored up the curving road with a menacing drainage ditch at my right side. I was beginning to breathe at an unacceptably accelerated rhythm. My mind sent instructions. Don't fight your body. At a gas station intersection, I got off the bike under an aromatic eucalyptus tree. I grabbed a leaf, crushed it, taking a few deep whiffs. If cycling takes off in La Paz, I'll recommend that they put oxygen masks at gas stations next to the air pumps. I wondered how much oxygen I needed to fill up.

I now decided to break the most important of the Ten Commandments: Thou shalt not push thy bike up a hill.

The incredible shrinking brain

I reasoned that the primary culprit was the altitude rather than the gradient, since my legs were holding up while my breathing had skipped off the map. I'd been in La Paz for less than a week, not enough time for my body to complete its task of producing larger and more numerous red blood cells, not enough days for my hemoglobin to activate its expanded oxygen distribution capacity. As I pushed, I considered the relationship between aging and adjusting to oxygen-deprived high altitudes. Supposedly old farts like me should need less oxygen because our brains are shrinking. That's what the blogger Tusker Geografica suggested in "Aging and Altitude": "...some doctors who specialize in high altitude medicine suggest that older people can tolerate altitude better because as we age our brain shrinks, requires less oxygen, and has more room in which to swell when inflamed."

Evidently I should thank my incredible shrinking brain, for at no point did I feel the most common symptom of Acute Mountain Sickness (AMS): a headache.

Even when I nearly collapsed in front of the old-age asylum, my head was as serene as Walden Pond. Could this lack of headaches be a sign of encroaching dementia in a shrinking brain? Brain atrophy, the loss of brain cells!

Should I be longing for a good old headache? My thoughts were not clear on this subject. After one block I got tired pushing, got back aboard and the pedaling now seemed easier than the pushing, until I would run out of gas, get off and start pushing again. In fact, pushing the bike at this altitude seemed nearly as strenuous as pedaling. But it involved different muscles, so the ride-push-ride-push method was diversifying my fitness routine, or so I assured myself. The macho in me retorted that no excuse could erase the embarrassing image of an old man pushing a green bike up a steep hill.

Trevor Ward's *The Guardian* bike blog asks: "If you've run out of gears on a steep slope, surely it makes sense to hop off the bike and push? So why is it considered the ultimate cycling heresy by many?" (16 Jan 2015)

Ward writes that under such circumstances, it's a no-brainer to walk the bike for awhile. "You are still progressing under your own steam, but using a different set of leg muscles...You could even argue that, compared with a cyclist using such performance-enhancing, technical trickery as a triple chain ring and dinner plate-sized, 34-tooth sprocket, your achievement was purer." I considered asking Aniceto to replace my cheap gears with a triple chain ring and dinner plate-sized, 34-tooth sprocket. Doping seemed like a more pleasurable option.

According to the physics blog, *Stackexchange.com*, "In principle, you can have gearing such that riding uphill can require less 'effort' than pushing the bike uphill." I prepared myself in case anyone came up to ask me why I was pushing the bike. I'd explain that pushing was "the interval" in interval training. Or I'd quote the former director of the Institute of High Altitude Medicine, who implored me to show great respect for the merciless altitude, where I get only 60 percent per breath of the oxygen compared to what I take in back home at the banks of the Seine River.

I may lose a few cycling purists at this point, but I made it to the Strongest stadium, 20% pushing and 80% pedaling. Good news: beyond the stadium I sighted paved residential streets that would allow me a checker-boarding reprieve. The Aymara town of Huayllani, "only" 100 meters above The Strongest stadium, looked attainable for my next outing.

I bowed in homage to the former Strongest football player Ramiro Castillo, who in 1997 as captain of Bolivia's national team, could have led his fellow players to a victory over Brazil in the final of the prestigious Copa América tournament had he not committed suicide several hours earlier. I was covering football for the newspaper Bolivian Times, but journalistic objectivity had not stopped me from becoming a fan of the Afro-Bolivian Ramiro Castillo.

The Brazilians and my bike-pushing strategy

It's worth noting that strategically, the Brazilians did the equivalent of my pushing the bike! They'd studied their high altitude medicine and knew they could not outrun the Bolivians in La Paz. So they stayed back in a purely defensive position, letting their opponents shoot away against a hopelessly clogged area in front of the goal. This high altitude strategy paid off. With a single breakaway, Brazilian star Ronald dribbled the ball the length of the field and put it in the goal. Final score: Brazil 1, Bolivia 0.

During the game, I could not help but reflect on Castillo's suicide by hanging. It came during a severe depression, linked by the press to the death of his 7-year-old son to hepatitis three months earlier. International football fans would always remember Pelé and Maradona, but who, outside of Bolivia, was going to remember Ramiro Castillo?

I had a personal connection with clinical depression. In two cases of students of mine, one back in California and the other in France, I'd participated with ad hoc teams of friends in offering attractive alternatives to suicide. In both cases, we failed. I cannot grasp the precise border between the profound sorrow that all parents would experience with the death of a child and the biological disease of clinical depression. I understand that Ramiro had failed in earlier attempts at suicide, as had my two students. Solidarity and friendship were not enough to stop them from their ultimate act.

In his *Spark: the Revolutionary New Science of Exercise and the Brain* (2013), Dr. John J. Ratey, professor of psychiatry at Harvard Medical School refers to patients whose severe depression has all but disappeared after they started to cycle. Greg LeMond, three-time winner of the Tour de France, gave the book a thumbs up.

In his Ted Talk, Dr. Ratey lent support to any form of exercise as mental health and brain therapy, so I plan to ask him if pushing a bike up a hill would qualify. The daily struggle up a hill could possibly help staving off Alzheimer's or Parkinson's but the magical downhill return did wonders for psychological renewal.

On my way down, I had a direct view of the 4,000 meter-high Altiplano (high plain), far in the distance, the other end of this immense hole in the earth. I wanted more of these gravity-assisted ego-enhancing descents. On the way down, mysterious recesses of my body that had managed to survive unaltered from the 1960s came to the surface, and for nearly a half hour, I became a 20-year-old.

As a reward for this replenishing morning, I decided to take two days off from the test of climbing to Huayllani and move directly to my second challenge: the splendidly perilous descent from El Alto to La Zona Sur.

CYCLING ON THE WORLD'S MOST DANGEROUS ROAD

When it was the main road beginning at the pass above La Paz at 4,600 m altitude (15,100 ft) and ending at a river town 9,000 feet below, you could argue that the Cumbre-Coroico was the most dangerous road in the world. Hairpin turns are lined with crosses where buses, trucks and mini-vans went off the narrow dirt ledge they call a road, plummeting into a bottomless ravine.

Today, with a newer parallel highway to the tropical resort town of Coroico, the old road has become the theater for splendid "gravity-assisted" cycling tours through various travel agencies, including the pioneer, Gravity Tours. The Road-of-Death tours are a magnet for tourists from around the world, professionally-accompanied excursions with safe thrills, rolling down through a luxuriant green cloud forest, on solid mountain bikes with the best brakes in the world, prepared for each trip by perfectionist mechanics.

When the new road first opened for circulation, Martha and I took a 7-hour "stroll" down the old road. I followed up our hike with an article in which I predicted that the road of death would become a great hiking attraction. I missed by one letter, needing a "b" instead of an "h." Today, Road of Death is an effective marketing phrase for one of the world's great bike tours.

For my maiden bike descent in La Paz, I chose a road that may be more dangerous than the original road of death. I refer to the Llojeta highway that descends from El Alto at 4,000 m down to the polluted Choqueapu River, merging into the Costanera Highway and ending up in the Zona Sur at Plaza Humboldt, nearly 800 meters below. That's a 2,600 foot drop.

When I visited the La Paz architect in charge of future cycling paths (ciclorutas), she told me that the Llojeta road was too steep for a bike path. To prove it, she showed me the frightening gradient calculations on her computer screen. Though much shorter in distance, the Llojeta road was steeper in many segments than the more famous road of death.

Add the dangers of urban traffic to the plummeting descent. Taxi and truck drivers elude the cost of the toll road from the El Alto Airport to the center of La Paz by using Llojeta as their alternate route. They're not used to seeing bicycles on their road and descending cyclists need to prove to each intimidating driver that we too have a right to the road, by waving and establishing eye contact. The more famous road of death is mostly free from motor vehicles. Before my departure, my wife's family ganged up on me with a litany of logical reasons to not cycle down this road. I could go over the precipice. I could get run over by a drunk truck driver or a joy-riding motorcyclist. I could be assaulted and robbed by the local hill dwellers.

I could hit a pothole and be vaulted directly forward into the cemetery below, thus compressing the two-step process of death-and-burial into a single more practical procedure.

I responded that I'd already prepped on a shorter but comparable downhill trip. I reported to them that the 40-block descent from the Valley of the Spirits to San Miguel was relatively easy because the road through Chasquipampa was wide enough for my own semi-private lane, but especially thanks to the speed bumps, which prevented a driver from barreling by irresponsibly. The Llojeta road also had speed-bumps, I assured them, not mentioning that in certain parts of the route was a parallel drainage ditch, preventing a bike rider from swerving off the road in case of an emergency.

Mixed-mode transportation

The plan was to travel up to El Alto via Teleférico, hoisting my bike into the Green Line station at Irpavi at the bottom end of the line, then transferring to the Yellow Line, whose uppermost station is in the Ciudad Satellite neighborhood of El Alto. Mi Teleférico's César Dockweiler, Executive Director of the enormously successful network of public aerial cable lines, is not only a former air force pilot and accomplished economist but a committed cyclist as well.

The only minor annoyances of getting into the cable cars involved carrying the bike up the 30 steps to the Green Line platform and then hoisting it over the turnstile. It's not in their job description but sometimes friendly agents will actually help lift the bike over. (After the fact, it was encouraging to learn that the Teleférico will add special doors for the handicapped to bypass the turnstiles, with cyclists allowed to pass through those doors.)

According to a tweet by Dockweiler, on 2 September 2018, a record was broken, with 13,083 bicycles traveling in Teleférico cabins, as part of the "Car-Free Day of the Pedestrian and Cyclist." The awesome Teleférico ride could never be duplicated by Disneyland and no theme hotel in Las Vegas could get away with an imitation. On the silent climb, we nearly scraped the hillside shantytowns, looking down on a rough life in an even rougher terrain, with precarious hairpin walking paths as well as brightly-painted outdoor staircases serving as human-energy elevators. The aerial cabin also glides over a few haunting voids in the cliffscape that serve as reminders of violent, rainy season landslides.

Once arrived at the last stop of the Yellow Line, I took a peak through the picture windows of a panoramic restaurant, an incongruous combination of fried chicken shop and upscale lookout café. The view was complex enough for one to remain gawking for an entire day. I could even pick out a street corner near our apartment, 650 meters below.

For you to grasp what this is all about, just stand on the rim of the Grand Canyon and imagine that a city of a million inhabitants had settled in below. On other occasions I would hang out at the Yellow Line terminal café and chat with real *ciclo-viajeros*. It's become a hangout for modern-day bike-packing hippies who are cycling across the entire continent. I met a Dutch guy who was on the way to Patagonia. He'd begun in Alaska! In comparison, my descent on the Llojeta road looked like mere child play.

I carried the bike down the 30 steps and skirting the edge of a precipice, I felt the luxury of cycling on a flat road! Whoopee! El Alto! The do-it-yourself city of El Alto had sprung up one red brick at a time, as a receiving area for internal-immigrants from rural territories. It's the most indigenous city of Bolivia, mainly Aymara speakers, recently reconstituting itself as an architectural competition space for builders of Cholets, the colorful and hyper-imaginative Chola/indigenous-modern chalets. These structures blend diverse roots leading back to both Atahuallpa, the last Inca emperor, and the renaissance Chateau de Chambord. Living on a flat plateau, El Alto residents are far more likely to use a bike to get around than the Paceños in the deep canyon city below.

The stray-dog trainer

The only danger on the street in this part of El Alto leading to the Llojeta road is a hyperactive population of stray dogs. Back in the '90s, when running laps around a La Paz football field, I educated the strays by carrying rock in hand. This was enough for them to keep their barking at a distance. Eventually the dogs and I became friends, but here in El Alto, my credentials as stray-dog trainer made no impression on the barking canines, who seemed very much in touch with their wolf ancestry.

On my bike I could carry neither rock nor stick, so only my pointed shouts might keep these grungy canines at bay. I tensed up. I could see their teeth shining in the unfiltered sun. Why weren't they backing off as they usually do? I slowed down, trying to show them I was cool. "Cool," I said. Eventually one of them bowed and turned away, and he must have been the leader of the herd because the others followed. Once I began the long descent, strident trucks replaced the dogs as the primary danger. In La Paz it's easier to train a stray dog than a stray driver.

Here was the great artistic contradiction: my eyes, which should have partaken of breathtaking views of the snow-peaked Cordillera and the roadside precipice, were employed instead to establish eye contact with motorists sharing the road, as well as to concentrate on the irregular asphalt below my wheels, in order to spot lethal potholes before it was too late. Potholes or no, I needed to stay in my lane in order to avoid a Mr. Magoo situation in which I would roll down the hill merrily, merrily, leaving in my wake a pile up of mini buses and trucks.

At one point I sensed the brakes were overheating and I found a way to exit the road in front of a makeshift ledge that served as a lookout. I let the brakes cool off, took a swig of glacier water, and finally had a chance to contemplate the knife-like outcrops in the gorges, the mountains behind them and the unfettered and chaotic urban development in their shadows. Around each hairpin turn, the road would suddenly dip, and I tensed up at the possibility that the next dip around the bend would be so steep as to send me reeling. To my right, partly-constructed red-brick mini-convenience stores would sometimes block my view of an upcoming curve so that I could not predict what was waiting for me around the blind bend: a sudden pothole, a sharp dip in the gradient, a grungy, bike-chasing dog.

I had a purpose: to lend my humble support to local bicycle activists in proving to La Paz highway architects that cycling such roads as a commuter is possible. Along the way I tested my imagination as to how and where a bike lane might be etched in, designating certain sections which would require a sign with big red letters: Walk your Bike: Pied à terre as it's announced in precarious portions of French bike paths. I would later meet a bike mechanic at Gravity Tours who used this same road to get to work. A new Llojeta line of the Pumakatari bus now allowed a commuter from El Alto to ride a bike down into the city and then put it on a bus rack for the return.

Once past the cemetery, the gradient diminished enough for me to cruise with ease, enabling me to enjoy the rugged terrain and the emergent neighborhoods within it. I made it to Plaza Humboldt in a gravity-induced sensation of invincibility. But then the final segment was upon me, an uphill sector to our apartment, 100 meters higher in altitude, precisely when the bombastic sun had begun to overwhelm my cancer- prone skin, letting me know that my invincibility had been a brief illusion.

REVELATION AT THE END OF THE WORLD

It took two more tries to make it to Huayllani, and then I went back and did it a second time, over an alternate route, a packed dirt road skirting the canyon wall. Either I was getting stronger or, once away from housing and motor vehicle traffic, the packed dirt road gave me extra psychic energy, for I did less pushing and my pedaling was more fluid.

I had a lot more conditioning ahead of me in order to catch up with Bolivian cyclists who climb the Road of Death, including a woman by the name of Mirtha Muñoz who has done the 65 kilometer charity ride from 4,430 feet in Yolosa until the Cumbre pass at 15,100 feet, roughly the same gradient as the much shorter trip from our apartment to Huayllani. I mention Mrs. Muñoz because she's done the climb on multiple occasions as she neared the age of 70! To equal her splendid feat in our own neighborhood, I'd have to do 12 consecutive trips to Huayllani.

Once an agricultural village, Huayllani was suffering from creeping, peri-urban gentrification. But the geography beyond Huayllani was so incongruous (knobby phallic stone formations, near vertical mountainsides with cavernous fissures) that the road came to an end of what John Wayne would have called a box canyon. In our populated world, with everything sprawling out, it is increasingly difficult to find endings. This was one of them. I could now claim that I had cycled to an end of the world.

The return home, 6 kilometers all downhill, was empowering, as usual. For 6 kilometers once again I morphed into an immortal college geography student. I later discovered that my repeated climbs were a slow-motion beginning of what they call "everesting." Everesting is a defiant challenge in which a bike rider climbs and descends any selected hill multiple times, in order to cumulatively climb 8848 meters (the elevation of Mt. Everest). To accomplish this feat, I'd have to do the Huayllani climb 29 times. The snow-covered Illimani that presides over La Paz is "only" 6,492 meters, which means only 22 climbs to Huayllani for the local version of everesting.

On a subsequent minibus visit to Huayllani, I found a dirt side road and walked it to an alternate end of the world, where I found two companion villages. Housing was going up there, helter-skelter, with subsistence farming plots in between. At the door of a small tienda, a type of general store on a wild-west main street, I asked a man standing in front if this was the last village, or if there were any populated areas beyond. "This is it," he answered, in English! In an American accent! Had I passed through the curvature of space, ending up in the wild coyote-inhabited hills above Irvine, California?

He told me he was from southern California. I asked him what he was doing in a part of Bolivia that even most Bolivians had never heard of.

"See that house down there?" He pointed past a motley crew of stray dogs, to an example of modern Bolivian minimalist architecture, out of context with the rutty dirt streets around it. Here and there, other attractive houses were going up, still in skeletal form. "That's my house." "But why here?" I asked.

"This is my American Dream. I would never have been able to afford a house like that in Orange County."

HOW TO CREATE A BIKE LANE, MAYBE

Wherever I go, I offer unwanted advice about the bicycle as transportation. In Irvine, California, in my role as grandfather, father and father-in-law, I've asked why city officials do little or nothing to encourage commuters to use their admirable network of bike lanes. Why not have a bike-to-school program? Why not subsidize employees who cycle to work, or who take their bikes into the Metrolink commuter train to work elsewhere? I've badgered the Irvine Shares the Way program to add these measures.

What I observed in Irvine was an occasional fashion parade of Mamils (Middle aged men in Lycra) through the bike lanes, bright striped helmets and jerseys streaming by, pockmarked with logos. A dazzling spectacle, for sure, but none of these carefree guys were on their way, car-free, to the office. In Clichy, just outside of Paris, I'd been part of a loose-knit team that harassed the previous and current mayors about installing a bike-bus-only corridor along the main Avenue Jean Jaurès, the one-way thoroughfare from suburbs to Paris. The project had stalled when local shopkeepers opposed the removal of parallel parking in front of their boutiques.

The bus-bike corridor was finally established in 2017. It was wide enough so that even if a delivery truck parked for a drop-off, there was still room to cycle around the truck without entering the stream of traffic. A half year later, I surveyed local boutique owners as to whether the elimination of parallel parking had hurt their business. The unanimous response was "Not at all." But after her "not-at-all," a clothing store owner added that she detested the bike-bus corridor "because I can no longer park at my shop and it's exorbitantly expensive to park elsewhere."

I also took my contentions to a City of Paris transport meeting in the renaissance-style Hotel de Ville (City Hall), in this case voicing support for the city's motorized-traffic-reduction policies, amidst car lobbyists repackaging themselves as friends of the environment. And in La Paz, Bolivia, a city with bike lanes prominent only in virtual urban planning documents, I exercised my rights as a part-time resident to ask when the first cicloruta would be established. Why not experiment with any one of the bike lanes in their mock-ups, connecting to shopping, workplaces, and transport stations?

Back in 2016, I learned from multiple reliable sources that decision makers within the La Paz City Hall, though very much in favor of a bicycle infrastructure, were reluctant to get the job done, for two compelling reasons: (a) the drastically contorted topography and (b) anarchistic motor traffic. They feared that by actually installing bike lanes, accidents might be precipitated. With their Ciclovía Activa (Sunday bike gatherings on closed- off streets) and their encouragement of Masa Crítica activists, the hearts of city officials were clearly on the right side.

Having confronted cycling in La Paz, I understood the reticence. So I took to the roads to carve out the least dangerous and most practical cycling corridor. If nothing else, my two-wheel surveying might encourage less-challenged municipalities around the world to do the right thing. The steeply-sloped Llojeta road was doable, but imagining myself in a position of authority, I could see myself balking before enormous safety concerns. After trying three potential routes, I was able to muscle through the most practical corridor between the upper La Paz business district and La Zona Sur, the city's two major commerce-residential- university centers.

Given certain narrow but obligatory segments along the Choqueyapu river gorge, implanted on a narrow ledge between river bank and towering cliffs, part of my proposed bike lane would have to be inserted on a non-residential sidewalk. Granted, this stretch of sidewalk is almost never used by pedestrians, but nevertheless, I'd had negative experiences in Paris on bike lanes embedded in pedestrian territory.

Even with Parisian sidewalk bike lanes allowing for adequate parallel pedestrian space, many strollers innately sense the bike lane to be part of their turf. As a result, such bike lanes might be more dangerous for the bike rider than cycling in the flow of car traffic. Perhaps bike lanes should never be placed on a sidewalk? I'm not sure. Errant pedestrians multitasking with their cell phones may be as unstoppable as the blowing wind.

But to conceive of a continuous bike lane connecting downtown La Paz with the South Zone, a half-kilometer stretch would require the sharing of a sidewalk. I'd ridden the road parallel to that sidewalk behind belching buses. I've seen daredevil Paceño bike riders doing the same. But if you want to encourage new bike commuters who are rightfully fearful of heavy traffic on a narrow road, the only solution for continuity from beginning to end of the corridor would be this stretch of shared sidewalk. The solution would involve copying signs on the Boulevard Magenta sidewalk bike lane in Paris: Pedestrians have the right of way.

As I mentioned, my proposed bike corridor was parallel to the Choqueyapu River. Now covered up in its downtown segment to eliminate foul odors, the Choqueyapu was the main geological sculptor of the "hole" they call La Paz, with help from several other above-ground rivers or brooks and more than a hundred underground streams. Anyone who cycles this corridor regularly, as I have, must have developed a love-hate relationship with the Choqueyapu. It's a geological enabler, allowing us to get through. But once past Curva de Holguín (the entry into lower La Paz), it stinks.

Political will has been lacking for financing a complex clean-up of the mess. This exemplifies the goes-around-comes-around principal. Faulty sewage facilities, poor residents and makeshift manufacturers in the upper zones of the city allow for a wide array of disgusting liquids and solids to be dumped into the river and streams leading to it.

But the Choqueapu flows down to the wealthier south and the affluent Paceños who live in the Zona Sur, the same ones who lacked the vision to finance a clean up, have become the principal victims of the foul odors.

This may appear like a typical third-world river story. But prosperous countries have faced the same dilemma. Consider the Bièvre River in Paris. Never heard of it? That's because it too was covered up after being deemed uncleanable. Near the Austerlitz train station, La Bièvre ends its 35-kilometer route by seeping underground into the Seine. If global warming continues to escalate, there will be no more river-producing glaciers left in the Cordillera above La Paz and many of the rivers that chiseled out the eventual urban-canyon landscape will dry up.

Bicycle archeology

During my in-the-saddle explorations of La Paz, I discovered the remains of an old bicycle lane along the Costanera highway, part of this same center-south corridor: here and there a faded "bike lane" sign as well as dim road-surface paint visible only to the eyes of a bike rider. A magnificent discovery! I'm now waiting for some university to award me an honorary degree in archeology. Here was an attempt by a previous mayor three decades ago to encourage cycling. It was a well-chosen corridor, for I still use it and feel adequately removed from the highway traffic.

Current city officials recall this bike path as a failed experiment, and now fear similar "white elephants" if they construct new bike lanes destined to remain unused. But times have changed. This bike lane disappeared because it failed to connected with strategic destinations. Today the very same corridor connects with transit stations, universities and new commerce that did not exist back then.

How about calling this bike lane a protected historical monument and then restoring it with a little fresh paint?

A DAY WITH MASA CRITICA

In the Ile-de-France region, I belong to an activist cycling group called MDB (*Mieux se Déplacer à Bicyclette*). We celebrate an annual Convergence in which at least 4,000 bicycle riders converge on the center of Paris to spread the word that the bicycle is a joyous and non-polluting form of transport. MDB branches situated in smaller cities in the region sponsor more intimate Sunday morning bicycle gatherings.

In La Paz, I discovered a group similar to both MDB and Vélorution, called Masa Crítica La Paz, which is part of a worldwide network of activist cycling organizations that began in San Francisco. The concept of critical mass is based on a Chinese principle that you need a critical mass of pedestrians or bike riders in order to safely cross an intersection. Critical mass groups look at ecology as a celebration rather than a sacrifice.

I'd never expected to find a Critical Mass in La Paz, given the intimidating topography I've described in previous chapters. During the Spanish colonial period, Miguel de Cervantes applied, unsuccessfully, to be appointed Mayor of La Paz. If he lived in today's La Paz, Cervantes' character Don Quixote would exchange his old horse Rocinante for a bicycle and would attack the steep cliffs as if they were legendary monsters.

When I learned that on 4 February, 2018 Masa Crítica La Paz scheduled a Sunday group ride, in the midst of the rainy season, I signed up. The plan was to descend over tortuous routes from the Camacho Market in central La Paz to the Plaza Humboldt, 400 meters below, in a path parallel to the bike lane I had "designed." It seemed like a crazy idea, since the group of more than 50 would include children and beginners. Even "Mayor" Cervantes might have disapproved, although the real La Paz City Hall gives its blessings to Masa Crítica. This particular descent was easier for me than the one I did from El Alto on the Llojeta road, but riding with a large group is considerably more suspenseful than going it alone.

On a hazy morning I pedaled to the bus stop at 21st Street in San Miguel. The driver, dressed in indigenous chola fashion, with bowler hat, dark braided hair, and layered skirts, got off the bus to lift my bike on to the front rack. (Official Pumakatari policy: the driver must place a passenger's bike in the rack.) I'd never seen a traditional chola woman (or any woman) driving a bus in La Paz. I recalled the words of culinary labor activist Petronila Infantes, herself an indigenous woman: "In the 1930s, we were not even allowed to ride on a tram." No way to interview my driver during her work hours, but her name, Sara Quispe Mamani, and picture were published a few weeks later in a photo essay: (Eduardo Leal, "The Rise of Bolivia's indigenous 'cholitas' in pictures," *The Guardian*, 22 Feb 2018). .

I reflected that in La Paz it might be easier to end racism than to establish bicycle commuting. Hanging around Plaza Camacho before we began our collective ride, I chatted with many of the bike riders, none of whom seemed worried about the presence of beginners and children. A young man in a Superman tee-shirt showed me photos on his cracked cell phone of more complicated bike routes he'd done in the foothills of the Cordillera. If given the chance, no doubt this kid would try to climb Everest with his bike.

I spoke with a man who looked my age, more or less in his early 70s, but with the solid frame of a Lance Armstrong. Several women cyclists seemed equally athletic. If Masa Crítica consisted only of supermen and wonder-women, its influence over City Hall would not be enough to convince the authorities to establish bicycle routes for a less athletic public. The Lance Armstrong of La Paz assured me that by practicing climbs incrementally, anyone can learn to cycle up hills. I longed to meet that "anyone." I wanted to be that anyone.

Guardian angels

We took off slowly at 10:20. The guardian-guide heading the peloton was Alex Franck. Alex once felt hounded by the Angel of Death. He never knew when this personification of death would reappear: at the exit of the famous Black Market, at the edge of the Choqueyapu river, in the lobby of the modern office building where he worked. His doctor told him he had no more than five years to live, given his complex and grave heart condition. After leaving the doctor's office, Alex went and bought a bicycle.

He practiced riding up hills, incrementally, and later organized a daring group called Illimani Biking Bunch (IBB). Illimani, the emblematic snow-capped mountain overlooking La Paz from 6,438 meters was IBB's symbol of defiance. Recall the gravity-assisted tours plunging down the Road of Death. Well, Alex has ridden the Road of Death in reverse: uphill, 2,000 meters higher, as part of a charity event sponsored by another daring biking group, Los Huanca.

After having gradually strengthened his aerobic resistance, new tests showed that Alex's health indicators had improved enough for the Personification of Death to stop hounding him at every intersection. If film director Ingmar Bergman were still around, he could use Alex's story for an alternative ending to his classic film, *The Seventh Seal*.

The guardian-guide protecting us from the rear was Mariana, who has masters degrees in urban studies, anthropology and psychology. In Ecuador, Mariana got to know a feminist group called the Carishinas, which assigned a *madrina* for each new bicycle commuter. Through this group, which empowers women through cycling, Mariana learned to master the art of bicycle commuting. She has continued her Urban Studies on two wheels.

Other guardian angels blocked traffic at intersections to assure us safe passage, and then sped past the peloton to intersections ahead of us to protect us once again. This was the same tactic used by my Paris-region group MDB for its Convergence events.

With its rigorous discipline, Masa Crítica La Paz earned the support of Ramiro Burgos, Secretary of Municipal Mobility, who has worked on a three phase plan to cultivate cycling in this unlikely geographic context.

1. Ciclovía Activa. "The use of the bicycle has been disappearing as the streets become more insecure and youth are distracted by electronic games," Burgos told me. "By closing two main routes for the Sunday morning bicycle gatherings, we are reawakening the bicycle culture."

2. Phase two is to establish pilot cycling routes, as a starter, identifying streets with lower traffic levels and lesser gradients.

3. Establish a network of ciclorutas, well integrated with intermodality so that bike riders can connect with public transport for the most difficult gradients.

As we descended through the historic bourgeois neighborhood of Sopocachi, a sweet drizzle settled upon us. As we halted briefly along Avenida 6 de Agosto I picked out Daniel Ardiles on the sidewalk, a feature newscaster on the ATB-TV Channel. I stopped to shake hands with him. (He would later invite me to an extended interview on his morning TV program, with footage of the Masa Crítica event.)

We crossed one of the Triplet Bridges in single file: below was the deep Choqueyapu gorge and above were precarious urbanized cliff sides, threatened each rainy season by the revenge of Mother Earth. Over the railing of the bridge I picked out the entrance to the Mallasa canyon to the south, framed by two burnt-red-stone bluffs. Far above us, cabins of the Yellow Teleférico line passed by mutely, also in single file: two silent processions crisscrossing at different levels of thin air.

As we descended on a narrow curve amidst these incongruous juxtapositions, I mulled over three indispensable factors for a livable city. One prerequisite was mixed-mode commuting, where bikes are allowed on public transportation, a victory of the Masa Crítica activists, in conjunction with favorably-minded public transportation administrators.

More difficult is the aggressive implementation of bicycle routes. The dialogue between bike advocates and the municipality is captive to a chicken-or-the-egg scenario: which comes first, bike lanes that should attract increasing numbers of bicycle commuters or a critical mass of cyclists convincing the authorities to build in the bike lanes? In a normal city, the bike lanes can come first, but in La Paz it's a simultaneous chicken and egg prerequisite.

Finally, already etched in the plans of the Programa de Centralidades Urbanas, directed by Paola Villegas, the development of self-sufficient neighborhoods, where local services are duplicated so that lengthier commutes to the grotesquely congested historical downtown are no longer necessary. Shorter purposeful bike trips allow for targeted bicycle lanes.

La Paz has delineated 19 different "centralities" for its million inhabitants, each one intended to have its own cultural centers, green areas, local commerce, and public service offices of government and municipal organisms. Villegas calls this an "eco-efficient system" in which pedestrians and bike riders begin to replace motorized vehicles. Our procession stopped in Obrajes, one of these centralities. A retired couple, hand in hand, approached me. Moved by our colorful bike parade, the man proclaimed: "What a thrill to see you all pass by. You have the right philosophy!"

I recalled my visit to the Oficina de Centralidades, where I found the bicycle of Ivan Asturizaga, Villegas' assistant, parked in the hall. Ivan is an example of Sí se puede! He explained: "The route from my home in Alto Obrajes to my job here in Sopocachi is about 2.3 kilometers, which I do round trip twice a day, for more than 9 kilometers per day. The trip begins in Alto Obrajes, which means crossing the emblematic Puentes Trillizos (Triplet Bridges) in order to then ride up the congested Arce Avenue." (I've been there, participated in the daily danse macabre between pedestrians and mini-buses.)

"In spite of risking my life in a city that still has no adequate bicycle infrastructure and whose topography defies the imagination," Ivan continued, "since I've been doing this commute by bicycle, I feel stronger and more energetic and the morning cold is no longer so piercing."

In the former Transport Office, now called Office of Mobility, I'd also found parked bicycles, one of which had a license plate: +Love --Motor.

Arriving at the Plaza Humboldt destination of this Masa Crítica procession, I began to believe that the bicycle as transport in complicated cities like La Paz is not a far-fetched reverie, that in smog-infested urban centers around the world, pedestrian and bicycle transportation can gradually replace the motor vehicle. Impossible dream? A few days later, a civic strike paralyzed all motor vehicle transportation in much of the city. In my neighborhood a joyous silence settled in. For the first time, I heard my own footsteps. Residents on liberated street corners hung out together without the fumes, recapturing their rightful space, and in some cases, meeting their neighbors for the first time.

I became eye-witness to the possibility that the good news you can read on the carfree.com website could spread to unlikely cities around the world. That morning, with news of the transport strike shaking radios at breakfast tables, hundreds of citizens left their homes on bicycles, pedaling to their jobs, or to the Green Line of the Teleférico for mixed-mode transport that would lift them over the toughest climb.

Mothers and fathers occupied the usually congested Avenida Ballivián, teaching their daughters and sons to ride a bike. Late afternoon I watched employees cycling back uphill on this same main avenue on their way home. I took advantage of the clean air and transparent silence to practice a future Cicloruta that I'd seen in diagrams in the urban plans of both Ramiro Burgos and Paola Villegas. The clean air made climbing much easier, so much that I didn't have to stop and push.

(Some material in this chapter previously appeared in Spanish, in Suburbano.net and in French, in Roue Libre.)

METABOLIC LIBERATION: FINDING YOUR NAHUAL

You can find your nahual and feel good again: With help from a character from Nobel Prize winning novelist, Miguel Angel Asturias

Can we recover from more than a century of the technological fixation on eliminating the use of our natural metabolic energy? My nephew takes the elevator instead of one flight of stairs. I have children who drive to the supermarket for minor purchases instead of walking. Donald Trump has used a motor-powered golf cart on the green, in order to avoid taking a few steps. I've seen neighborhoods in Livonia, Westchester, and North Hollywood with no sidewalks, where people from behind living room curtains call the Neighborhood Watch if they see someone suspiciously walking on the street. I've seen healthy young men and women using garage door openers instead of their arms, in order to drive to health clubs instead of cycling there, in order to go nowhere lifting weights and riding a stationary bike.

The descendants of the Mayans might see us as losing contact with our Nahuals, our intimate animal ancestors.

For years I was a neighbor of the great Guatemalan novelist, Miguel Angel Asturias, my apartment near Rue de Pyrénées, and Asturias in his grave in the Père-Lachaise Cemetery, eastern Paris. In the Asturias novel Men of Maize, a character named Correo-Coyote, a long-distance mail carrier, would morph into his nahual, a coyote, in order to cover long-distance rural routes.

I stand before your tomb, Señor Asturias, to let you know that I am now taking your character literally, and not simply as a Mayan myth or figure of magical realism. I am searching for my own nahual, in order to cover long distances by bike. The nahual represents our own particular animal heritage, and genome research proves that we do still have such an identity: our animal identity as a quadruped. (Humans and mice, for example, share nearly 90% of DNA!) We've gained much in evolving into bipeds but through this transformation we have lost a lot as well.

When we discover our nahual, we recover part of what we've lost, without giving up what we've gained. Like the experts who help you find your genealogical roots, I can help you travel back to a more distant and nebulous past, in order to recover your own nahual, with the difference that my service is for free. We often use the word "animal" to insult a rival. But contrary to humans, animals rarely kill for the sake of killing. They kill when they are hungry, and not their own species, at least not like the guy who shot down concert goers from his hotel window in Las Vegas, and they do not make "wars of choice." Strange contradiction: our animal nahual can humanize us.

One way to find your own nahual is to choose a means for covering ground with your two feet in coordination with your two arms. This can be by bicycle, roller blades or hiking with the use of walking sticks.

When animals move from one place to another, they usually do so with a practical purpose: hunting for food, finding water or searching for a mate. In the case of Correo-Coyote, he was a *chasqui*, who carried the mail to distant places. All over France I've seen bicycle-riding mail carriers who use all fours to deliver the correspondence, in the tradition of the Jacques Tati film, *Jour de Fête*.

According to paleontologist Sydney Savory Buckman, "We find in cycling, to a certain extent, a return to the movement of a quadruped because our arms have to do the support work and the body is not standing on its extremities but suspended like that of a quadruped, supporting itself from in front and behind." (*The Medical Magazine,* 1900).

In this quadruped position I feel a revival. The famous writer Emile Zola felt similar renewal back in the time of Buckman. Once Zola discovered the bicycle, he gathered the courage to publish his famous letter, J'accuse, in which he defended General Dreyfus against the ruling class antisemitism of the times. Also thanks to the bicycle, Zola became a macho: political audacity, sexual virility. Perhaps a literary critic could discover the naturalist Zola's nahual. My own nahual could not be the coyote since I do not enjoy eating meat. Among the quickest animal vegetarians we find the springbok of South Africa, the gnu (ugly critter and often victim of predatory felines) and the horse. Prior to the search for my nahual, I'd written various books on horse racing, and done so with organic pleasure, while never writing about any other animals. I've therefore deduced that my nahual is the horse.

I've shown you my method for recovering my nahual. I'm sure you have your own nahual and that it could be in your interest to uncover its identity. This is not an intellectual search. It is, above all, metabolic. (1) First, think back to your unconscious or subconscious acts, associating these acts with the most fitting animals, without consulting your rational side; (2) follow up by deciding which is your most appropriate means of propelling yourself, not involving the automobile, which would make your nahual the sloth.

Once you've identified your nahual, you will be putting a stop to the sedentary trend of allowing machine energy to replace the metabolic energy that enabled us to evolve in the first place.

(Some material in this chapter appeared previously in Spanish, at Suburbano.net)

WANTED: BICYCLE COMMUTER OR TRAVELER, UNBEATABLE JOB

I'm now hiring.

If you're committed to either commuting or touring by bicycle, you got the job. No drug test prior to hiring. No check of criminal record, no references required. Just start riding to work, even if you take your bike in public transportation part ways. Or begin taking vacations by bicycle. If you don't like cycling then do the same on foot, blending with public transportation, now known officially among urban specialists as "active transport". The only prerequisite is that this must be an activity you will enjoy. No applicant who considers this job a sacrifice will be hired. Neither altruism nor self-punishment is sustainable.

One car less, one step forward to cleaner air, and maybe curtailing global warming as well.

For the time being I cannot pay a salary. But your income will automatically improve by not using your car, and unless you do not fall within the statistical mean of medical research, your health and well-being will also improve. Once you join this enterprise, which began long before I hopped aboard, you'll receive an ecological bonus for recruiting new colleagues to use their bicycles or feet as transport.

If you decide to take the job, use this book as your employment manual. Pay heed to all the embarrassing mistakes in my own bike travels and you will avoid most potential misfortunes.

Sign here to waive your employer, me, from all responsibility for any one-of-a-kind fluke mishap, and initial your commitment to obeying all traffic rules in the spirit of the law.

X

PostScript

9 RANDOM MISHAP SCENARIOS (ADVANCED STRUCTURE FAILURE ANALYSIS)

1. Riding with your mouth open, a bee or wasp is swept inside your mouth.

2. Beneath some dry autumn leaves on the pavement are wet autumn leaves that cause you to lose your bearing.

3. You are aware that you should cross small curbs in the pavement perpendicularly, but a particular curb is hidden by an overgrowth of grass and you cross it at an angle, swerving out of control.

4. A pedestrian is text-messaging while walking and steps into the bike lane timing it perfectly to coincide with your speedy arrival.

5. You have tied your shoelaces meticulously but for some reason a loosened shoelace jams your pedal just when you are making a left turn in traffic!

6. Cycling over a well-packed dirt path, you suddenly hit a soft patch that feels like the sand at Santa Monica Beach, making you struggle in a panic to control the bike.

7. Within a bike lane, an errant child walks in your direction, seemingly making eye contact with you, and yet he still proceeds obliviously, directly into your path, no matter which way you decide to turn. I'm a father, I love kids, but pigeons are more dependable.

8. You get up early in the morning and cycle while singing "Sunday Morning Sidewalk," forgetting that the Saturday-night sidewalk was strewn with broken bottles from hardcore partiers.

9. By admiring a most beautiful view above, you fail to see a lethal pothole below, right in your path.

6 Atypical Bike Rides

We can discover thousands of one-of-a-kind cycling experiences around the world. Just for an appetizer, I'll mention six that I've done.

1. Cascais, Portugal. When you get off the train at this beach town, a half hour from Lisbon, you bump into a free bike service. Yes, a bike for free! You leave your ID or passport as security and pick it up when you return. It's a 20 km circuit, mainly protected bike lanes, over magnificent palisades and past rugged beaches between Cascais and the surfing mecca, Praia de Guincho, which is framed by jagged stone bluffs. Along the way you pass the former cave turned stone arch, Boca de Infierno. The municipal biCas is a very basic single-speed bike, with no lock or helmet, and you'll hit several hills, not steep but long enough for a reasonable workout. At the lookouts along the way you'll find free potable water. Pick up your bike early since it must be returned by 7pm.

2. Valencia and Santa Clarita, California. This looks like a cookie-cutter southern California suburb until you discover, hidden within, a network of paseos and trails, where you can bike, run, or walk, for much of the way under the cool shade of trees. Why is this unique? It is one of the few urban cycling circuits in Southern California where you are largely protected from the battering sun. The 30+ miles of Santa Clarita trails and Valencia paseos within the system either cross over or under major streets, which eliminates intersections but adds some healthy mild climbing as you wind your way between neighborhoods and shopping centers. You can make this a bike-hike biathlon by connecting with the Placerita Canyon State Park, where I've done an hour+ wooded climb that peaks at an awesome expansive view of the San Fernando Valley. There are two Metrolink stations in the Santa Clarita area, where you can board the bike-car of a train.

3. Cárdenas, Cuba. Cárdenas is within 11 km of the bridge leading to Cuba's emblematic beach resort, Varadero. If Varadero represents mass tourism, colonial Cárdenas is all about authenticity. The two main modes of transportation in this "Non-Varadero" are bicycles (private) and horse-drawn carriages (public). In fact, Cárdenas has a giant statue of a bicycle in one of its roundabouts. In the 1990s, cycling came to the rescue as the primary mode of transport in Cuba, when, as a result of the fall of the USSR, the oil spigot to the island was shut off.

Cárdenas is nicknamed the Chicago of Latin America because of its neat street grid where it's impossible to get lost. I stayed with a family in Cárdenas and was able to use their Chinese-Cuban-made Flying Pigeon bike, legendary for its heaviness and instability. Cars do not flood Cuban roads and it's possible to cross the whole island without changing gear, though it's well worth visiting the mountains. (Bikes are also admitted in ferries out of Havana, and in my ferry rides, the majority of commuters were bike riders.)

4. Barcelona, Spain/Catalunya. Ranked number 11 amongst the best cycling cities in the world (Paris is 13th), Barcelona is top-ranked among Mediterranean cities by bike advocate Mikael Colville-Andersen's *Copenhagenize* website. Barcelona is atypical for three reasons.

First, it's so easy to cycle there! It's hard not to find a bike lane, and bike markings extend through intersections, which is not the case in Paris. My second reason is aesthetics. Contrary to most cities ranked above it, Barcelona offers cycling access to both lively beach-front and "entertaining" hills with a view, with eye-catching Gaudi buildings in between. Along the way you get a free Catalan lesson from the bike signs. Finally, Barcelona has begun a network of "superblocks", in which local access for motor vehicles is still permitted, but through traffic is not. The streets are designed to make drivers feel like they're encroachers, with narrow rights-of-way for cars. Almost all car traffic involves local residents or people with personal business on the block. (See *Streetsblog.org*)

5. Bruges, Belgium with its refreshing below-sea-level canal paths, and

6. La Paz, Bolivia taking your bike up in a breath-taking aerial cable car and then letting gravity take you back down: both are depicted within the body of this book.

21 ECLECTIC SOURCES

Among hundreds of informative and/or entertaining sources on cycling in the realms of transportation, health, and environment, I'll choose 21, in alphabetical order, apologizing in advance that so many valuable websites, books, articles and videos could not find a parking space in this list.

Bicycle Touring Pro, Youtube. Darren Alff films his international travels and along the way provides us with valuable tips on bicycle touring. Among cycling tour videos, *TheBicycleTouringPro* is best at making you feel right there, and Darren Alff chimes in from time to time with authentic and refreshingly unassuming philosophies.

Bike Blog gives *The Guardian* team of perceptive journalists the cycling edge over other newspapers, with Peter Walker, Laura Laker, Peter Kimpton, Andrew Gilligan, Carlton Reid and Kylie van Dam, to name just a few, covering issues relating to the bicycle as transport for commuting and touring, as well as the environmental implications.

British Medical Journal, "Association between active commuting and incident cardiovascular disease, cancer and mortality: prospective cohort study," 19 April 2017. Cycle commuting was associated with a lower risk of CVD, cancer, and all cause mortality with 263,450 participants in the study.

Carfree Cities at *carfree.com,* including the *Carfree Times* newsletter. Once you visit this website you'll be hooked. A wealth of ideas and images gathered by JH Crawford, author of *Carfree Cities* (2000) and *Carfree Design Manual* (2009), a book that offers new hope and insights for everyone who cares about where they live.

City Cycling, edited by John Pucher and Ralph Buehler, with 21 expert contributors. Eye-opening demographic research. Revealing developments in urban cycling with precision narrative and statistics revealing that bicycling as transport should not be limited to those who are highly trained, extremely fit, and daring enough to battle traffic on busy roads. A benchmark book that will stand the test of time, according to David Banister, professor of transit studies, University of Oxford.

Copenhagenize.com, Bicycle Culture by Design, ranks the top 20 large cities according to bicycle friendliness, informs, lobbies, and does consulting. Part of the package is the book *Copenhagenize: the Definitive Guide to Global Bicycle Urbanism* by Mikael Colville-Andersen. No one person has done more to spread the word about the glories of the bicycle as urban transport.

Critical Mass or similar groups. Google generically "bicycle organization" + name of city," for websites and facebook pages. No two bicycle association websites are alike with each one innovating in its own way, in the realms of joyous or militant special events, cycling tips, aesthetic ideas or lobbying. While part of an international movement, these groups begin by acting locally even in unlikely bicycle venues such as Nashville and Phoenix.

Degowth.org. Comprehensive and eclectic sources on living a richer life and nurturing the environment by consuming less. Serious studies on the flaws of GNP measurements, with a rich array of alternatives presented.

"Dutch bikers live six months longer," Utrecht University (22 June, 2015) in reference to research in the 11 June 2015 edition of *American Journal of Public Health*: "Dutch Cycling: Quantifying the Health and Related Economic Benefits" (Fishman, Schepers, Kamphuis)

FreewheelingFrance, website. Best English-language source for cycling in France. Breathtaking menu of self-guided tours and tips. Hard to find any other cycling country that blends a temperate climate, remarkable variations in geography, a network of mellow country roads and a visibly well-preserved historical context.

Guide for Fat Cyclists, published on the Average Joe Cyclist blog. Writes Joe Goodwill, "We need to reclaim the word "fat" as simply an adjective, not as a term that makes us feel ashamed or less worthy than people who happen to be not-fat. And definitely not as a word that makes us unworthy to be cyclists" and "A fat person who gets a lot of exercise may be healthier than a thin person who gets no exercise." A helpful blog for all citizen cyclists.

Illich, Ivan. *Energy and Equity*. Illich was a leading iconoclast of the 20th century, a visionary precursor of the degrowth movement, and above all, a defender of humanity against preconceived notions. This book is available for free in PDF files on line. Illich championed the bicycle as transport before it was popular to do so.

Jay Walljasper, editor of *Commons Magazine* and author of visionary books such as *The Great Neighborhood Book*, is an idea man who proposes real solutions for social ecology and environment with can-do optimism, a welcome antidote to doom-and-gloom rhetoric.

PeopleforBikes.org, website. Helps communities build better places for bikes, lobbies in our favor and provides a wealth of information and articles on trends and progress for cycling and quality of life. Excerpt from their "Why We Ride": "We ride for fun. We ride for fitness. We ride to get from here to there, to free ourselves from the daily grind, and to make our world a better place through bikes."

Reinventing Transport podcast, hosted by Paul Barter: *reinventingtransport.org,* with stimulating discussions and interviews on mobility and related themes, with international breadth and a wealth of sometimes wonky detail.

Sadik-Khan, Janette and Solomonow, Seth. S*treetfight: Handbook for an Urban Revolution.* As courageous commissioner of the NYC Department of Transportation (2007-2013) and with the valuable support of activist organizations, Janette Sadik-Khan transformed New York City's streets to make room for pedestrians, bike riders, buses, and green spaces. A model to follow.

Streetsblog , website: informing the movement to improve walking, biking and transit. News, innovation, social justice. Stunning videos and startling fact-based articles, such as "The Bible Belt Should Really Be Called The 'Carnage Corset' For Pedestrians" (23 Jan 2019) and "Self-Driving Car Makers Prepare To Blame Jaywalkers" (17 Aug 2018).

Todd Litman blog on *Planetizen* . Litman is founder and executive director of the Victoria Transport Policy Institute, an independent research organization dedicated to developing innovative solutions to transport problems. Litman's blog is a go-to source for improving transportation policy and practice.

Transportation Alternatives, website. Gets the job done in New York City and is a model for urban groups around the USA and abroad.

Tati, Jacques film, *Jour de Fête (The Big Day,* in English). Listed as one of the ten great bicycle films by BFI Film Forever, "follows the mishaps of a French rural postal worker, Fraçois, played by Tati himself. Under the influence of too much wine and after viewing a film about the modern methods of the US postal service at the village fair, he goes to extreme measures to speed up his own postal delivery. Slapstick hilarity ensues." (Many French cities, including mine, continue to have their mail carriers deliver by bicycle.)

350.org covers news and leads events around the world related to keeping fossil fuels in the ground and creating a just, prosperous, and equitable world built with the power of ordinary people. Not specifically focused on bicycle movements, *350.org* connects with bicycle groups by publishing inspiring testimonies.

Made in the USA
Las Vegas, NV
09 June 2021